# About the Author

Paul Roland is a qualified counsellor and teacher of mysticism and meditation. He also runs workshops in facilitating contact with angels and has studied meditation, spiritual healing, Buddhism and practical magic. He is the author of several books including *Kabbalah: A Piatkus Guide*, *Prophecies and Predictions*, *Revelations: The Wisdom of the Ages* and *The Complete Book of Dreams*.

# ANGELS

# ANGELS

## AN INTRODUCTION TO ANGELIC GUIDANCE, INSPIRATION & LOVE

## PAUL ROLAND

PIATKUS

This book is dedicated to
Michael and Joshua Roland, my own two angels
in this world

Disclaimer: The meditation exercises included in this book are designed for relaxation and developing self-awareness. However, anyone who has emotional or mental problems or who has had problems of this nature in the past should seek professional medical advice before attempting any of these exercises. The author and publisher accept no responsibility for any harm caused by or to anyone as a result of the misuse of these exercises.

© 1999 Paul Roland

First published in 1999 by
Judy Piatkus (Publishers) Ltd
5 Windmill Street, London W1T 2JA
www.piatkus.co.uk

Reprinted 2001

**The moral rights of the author have been asserted**

*A catalogue record for this book is available from the British Library*

ISBN 0-7499-2020-3

Designed by Sue Ryall

Set in 12.5/14 pt Perpetua
Typeset by Action Publishing Technology Limited, Gloucester
Printed & bound in Great Britain by
Mackays of Chatham PLC

# Contents

# Introduction

If you have no direct experience of angels you may think of these Divine discarnate beings in theological terms, which define an angel as a class of spiritual being, 'a Divine messenger'. One of the main aims of this book is to show that such conventional views are not only misinformed, but that they also limit our understanding of the nature and purpose of existence by imposing human values upon what is beyond human comprehension.

The personal experiences of angelic encounters described in the course of this book – many of which were related to me by students in my angel workshops and meditation classes – were certainly real for those who experienced them. In some cases the impression was so profound that it altered their perception of 'reality'. But spiritual and psychic experiences are largely subjective and for that reason it is not possible to say precisely what angels are, where they come from and what they do. I hope, however, that the experiences I have described, the exercises that I have included and the understanding that I have reached will help to dispel many of the myths and misconceptions surrounding the subject so that you can discover the true nature of the angels for yourself.

## Angelic Encounters

The one thing that most of the people who attend my angel courses want to know is: have I personally seen an angel? It is almost as if they will not believe what they suspect is true until someone else admits to having seen the same thing. The answer is yes, I have seen an angel, although not in the form I had expected, which helped to convince me that what I was seeing was not merely a product of my imagination.

It appeared on a clear, crisp winter night some years ago. I was standing in my back garden looking up at the stars when the thought of asking for angelic protection around my house idly passed through my mind. The next moment an awesome, gaunt-faced figure appeared highlighted against the sky. It didn't have any wings that I could see, but carried a formidable-looking sword, and to my surprise it didn't acknowledge me at all. It was as if I had glimpsed another reality existing in between the matter that gives the illusion of form to our physical world.

Curiously, for weeks after that experience my two-year-old son Michael (named after the archangel, of course) insisted on telling us about his invisible friend, 'Malakha'. It wasn't a mispronunciation of his own name as he could say that clearly enough, nor was it similar to the name of anyone else we knew. Then, while working on a book on the subject of Kabbalah (for Piatkus), I was reminded of the Hebrew word 'Malakh' (pronounced 'Malakha') which means messenger and was the named used in biblical times for an angel. From that day on my son never mentioned 'Malakha' again, perhaps because the message had been received.

## Angelic Assistance

These events are not the only basis for my belief in the existence of angels; I have a sense of their presence on a daily basis and I know that they have helped me when I requested their assistance. In fact, I consider this book to be proof of their intervention in my life, and its publication serves as an example of how the angelics function for our mutual benefit.

Before I was asked to write this book I was becoming increasingly tired of writing to tight magazine deadlines, and of the magazines folding just as the work was beginning to come in on a regular basis. I considered asking the angels for help with finding regular jobs, ideally writing books, which would give me the security of long periods of work. However, I did not feel it was 'right' to ask the angels for money, even if I was going to have to earn it. I believed that it was enough to practise what I preached in my meditation classes and angel workshops – that being a 'good soul', so to speak, would result in help. Well, I was helped, but only to the degree that ensured we just got by; as soon as money came in, it went out again.

I had two small children to keep, my wife was looking after them and was not able to work, so it was all down to me and I felt that I was working very hard without making any real progress. At this point my wife again suggested I ask the angels for financial help, and again I couldn't do it. Instead I found a literary agent and put my faith in her, but after nine months she had failed to find me a single job.

Curiously, when I did finally ask the angels, very specifically, for book work and lots of it, it came almost immediately. I was overwhelmed with offers from several publishers and a multi-national company who wanted me to teach meditation to their overworked employees, just as two of the three magazines I was then writing for ceased publication. It was almost as if the angels were demonstrating the laws by which they operate. Under 'normal' circumstances you might expect your fortunes to pick up slowly after changing your attitude or circumstances, but it was as if I had opened a cupboard marked 'angels' and the goodies that had been set aside for me over the years came tumbling out all at once. Since that time I have been working seven days a week, every week, and not because I want to, but because I have to. Now I know the meaning of the saying, 'Be careful what you ask for, you just might get it!'

There are dozens of other incidents in my life and those of my family and friends which I could cite to show how the angels have averted disaster or brought help at just the right moment, even though I had not consciously asked them for it.

Sometimes angelic assistance is not even given a sheen of synchronicity with which we could entertain doubt; it is almost as if we were being given the confirmation we unconsciously wished for. One example of this occurred when an elderly relative asked the angels to help relieve her of the strain of maintaining her extensive and rambling garden by helping her to find the money needed to have it landscaped. One hour later she received an unexpected phone call from a telephone company, informing her that they had just discovered they had been overcharging her for 20 years for rental on a second line that she did not have. In due course they reimbursed most of her money, just enough to have the garden landscaped as she had asked for.

But the incident that impressed me most was the overwhelming and quite unexpected response to my first angel workshop. In the weeks leading up to the first meeting I would get regular frantic phone calls from the lady who was helping me to organise it to say that people from miles around were asking if they could book seats. Some rang to say that they were hiring a minibus and would we guarantee them a place. It was quite remarkable, particularly as we hadn't advertised the meeting other than by a mailshot to various friends and a few small posters in local shops.

On the night over 70 people attended, most of whom were in their twenties and thirties, and some of whom had travelled two or three hours to get there. Many reported afterwards that they had experienced contact for the first time that night, and that they were no longer anxious about the 'unknown'. They each had different experiences during the meditations (some of which are included in this book) – some felt a presence, some felt heat, some saw light or colours, and one lady was stunned to be taken out of her body into the celestial realms that I had been describing. She later admitted to being quite anxious, not having experienced anything like it before, but then she told me that two of her deceased relatives had appeared beside her and told her that all was well and that they were there to protect and guide her.

I had no idea there was such an interest in angels, and certainly not in a tiny town on the Kent coast. Subsequent meetings were also well attended and the revelationary experiences continued. When I stopped to concentrate on my books and began teaching meditation at an adult education centre the experience was no less remarkable. On several occasions I used my angel meditations, but I rewrote the scripts to exclude the angelic element as the course was intended to help people cope with stress and the spiritual element was not required. To my surprise, however, one lady came out of the meditation in a euphoric state and told the class that she had just met an angel!

## Contacting Angels

You do not have to be a 'religious' person to appeal for help from the angels. Nor do you have to subscribe to a specific belief system, other than the belief which says that as a Divine being you have the right to ask for assistance from those who serve the universal life force, and you have the right to expect their help.

We allow so many negative messages into our consciousness, particularly from the sensation-hungry media, without considering the effects, yet we hesitate to call on the universal life force which sustains and nurtures us every day of our lives. Many people are reluctant to believe in angels or to contemplate the existence of the greater reality of which these celestial beings are a part. Rational thinking and religious dogma have been largely to blame for stifling our belief in such things, but over the course of this book I hope to dispel some of the myths and misconceptions that I believe have obscured the true nature of the angels from our sight for centuries. It is a truth which, as you might expect, is divinely simple. By following the guided meditations, used to considerable effect with students over many years, I hope you too will become aware of the presence of the angels in your life.

*Note*: In accordance with esoteric tradition I am obliged to point out that what follows is my personal interpretation of the invisible realms and their inhabitants as passed down to me by my teachers and filtered through revelation and personal experience. Each reader should weigh the truth of what follows for themselves and accept only what feels right for them.

## Helpful Hints for Successful Meditation

Relax but stay focused; don't be so eager to make contact with your angels that you fail to truly relax. You already have the contact that you seek. You now need to develop awareness of that contact, and that comes with learning to still the mind and listen more effectively. Don't try. Let go and let the angels draw closer.

Be patient. As with any form of exercise, the more you practise, the easier it will come. If you have not meditated before or are of a nervous nature, always remember that you are not going anywhere, so there is no need for anxiety. You are always in control and can end the exercise at any time. You are expanding your consciousness, your awareness and tapping latent inner resources for your own highest good. Remember the universal law that 'like attracts like'; no harm or negative influence will come to you if your intentions are of the highest. However, if you are uncomfortable at any point, simply count down slowly from ten to one in your mind and you will find that the anxiety disappears before you reach five. You can then rejoin the exercise.

At the end of every meditation it is important to ground yourself to regain your balance and sense of reality. There are a number of ways to do this, including drinking a glass of water, washing your face and hands with cold water, having a refreshing shower or taking a short walk, preferably in a natural environment such as a garden or park.

For practical purposes and to save you from having to refer continually to the text it is recommended that you record the scripts of the various exercises on to cassette, perhaps with a background of suitably inspiring music or natural sound effects to create a relaxing atmosphere.

The following exercise is designed to help you establish contact with each of the seven angels who are said to govern the chakras – the subtle energy centres in the human body. By connecting with these angels on a daily basis, ideally before breakfast and again before you go to sleep at night, you release vital energy which will balance, ground and protect you from negativity. It is particularly effective in stressful situations when you need to calm and centre yourself, and is useful in helping to settle the mind before sleep or after a disturbing dream. You can also use this exercise whenever you wish to establish a sacred space around yourself and open communications with the angels.

## EXERCISE: TUNING IN

☆ Make yourself comfortable with your back straight, your feet flat on the floor and slightly apart, and your hands on your thighs.

☆ Close your eyes and begin to focus on your breathing. Take slow, deep, regular breaths. Scan your body from the crown of your head to your toes for areas of tension. When you find a point of tension tense that muscle tighter and then relax it. When you have scanned your entire body take a very deep breath and sigh. This releases the remaining tension and allows the breath space inside your body.

☆ Now take slightly deeper breaths than usual, pausing at the top of the breath and at the bottom. Feel your body and muscles relaxing with each out-breath. When you feel sufficiently relaxed say to yourself, 'I am going to count from one to ten and when I reach ten I will be in a very deep state of relaxation and heightened awareness, in which I can communicate with my angelic guides and receive their love, light and healing energy for my highest good.'

☆ Visualise the number one and the colour red. Red is the colour of physical energy and corresponds to the vibrational frequency personified by the Angel Gabriel whose Hebrew name means 'Strength in God'. Absorb yourself in red and feel that every cell in your body is being revitalised and awoken to the life force.

☆ Visualise the number two and the colour orange. Orange is a blend of the red of physical energy and the yellow of the mental level, and corresponds to the emotions. It is governed by the Angel Uriel whose name translates as 'The Light of God'.

☆ Visualise the number three and the colour yellow. Yellow, the second of the primary colours, is symbolic of the revitalising, healing energy of the sun and of the intellect. Absorb yourself in yellow and become aware of its power to heal, to heighten the imagination and stimulate drive, confidence and ambition. Sense the presence of the Angel Raphael who governs this chakra and whose name means 'The Healing Power of God'.

☆ Visualise the number four and the colour green. Green is the colour of harmony and balance, of nature and of peace. It is symbolic of the boundary between the physical and spiritual realms. Imagine yourself surrounded in green and feel refreshed by the Angel Michael whose name means 'Like unto God'.

☆ Visualise the number five and the colour purple which is the colour most frequently associated with the third eye, the psychic 'sixth sense' located in the centre of the forehead between the eyebrows. This colour corresponds to the Angel Zadkiel whose name means 'Righteousness of God', which can be understood to refer to the quality of integrity.

☆ Visualise the number six and the colour violet. Violet is a transitional colour in practical, psychological and spiritual terms, being a blend of red (physical energy) and blue (the celestial realm). It is the colour associated with the Angel Samael whose name means 'Contraction of God', which can be understood as personifying the need for consolidation prior to change or rebirth in a new form.

☆ Visualise the number seven and the colour blue. Blue is the third primary colour and is the first of the spiritual colours. Blue rules over the passions and the mental processes, and is symbolic of unconditional, selfless love which has no compulsion to possess. It is the colour corresponding to the veil through which we pass when we surrender to the higher, Divine part of ourselves that has been called the Higher Genius, the Higher Self or the guardian angel.

☆ Visualise the number eight and the colour gold. Gold embodies heavenly glory and earthly power and as such was the chosen metal for sacred objects and the ultimate aim of the alchemists. It corresponds to the frequency of vibration personified by the Angel Raziel whose name means 'Secret of God'.

☆ Visualise the number nine and the colour silver. Silver symbolises intuition and corresponds to Zaphkiel, the angel of contemplation, whose name means 'Wisdom of God'.

☆ Finally, visualise the number ten and the colour white, symbolising the highest (crown) chakra, or subtle energy centre in the etheric body. This is the realm of influence governed by the Archangel Metatron whose name means the 'Spirit of the Presence'. As the highest of the archangels he acts in God's name, overseeing the progress of mankind. 'Experience' white; absorb yourself in this highest of colours from which all the other colours come. White is the protector, the light of the God-force. Imagine that you are drawing a circle of white light around you, below your feet and above your head, to protect yourself from the negativity of the physical world and to create a sacred space in which to work with your angelic guides.

☆ When you have completed your contact with the angels, return to waking consciousness gradually by counting slowly from ten to one. You can repeat the following affirmations as you do so to reinforce their positive message on the unconscious.

*When I awake I will be full of life and vitality, knowing that I am the living spirit within.*

*I am in harmony with life, nature and the cosmos.*

*I only think positive thoughts; I only feel positive feelings; I only hold positive attitudes that make me successful, happy and healthy. I know that with every breath I take my physical body is healthier, stronger and more vibrant. I am at peace within and this serenity and stillness will radiate outward to the outer conscious level. I have full control and complete dominion over all levels of my being.*

☆ Become aware of your breath. Become aware of your body sitting in the seat, and when you are ready, open your eyes.

# 1

# Angels Through the Ages

## Angels in the Ancient World

We cannot be certain where the idea of angels originated, but it seems likely that they evolved from the winged deities of Sumerian, Egyptian and Semitic belief. These beings were depicted and sometimes described as 'messengers of the gods', from which the word 'angel' is derived, after the Greek word *angelos* meaning messenger.

The earliest representation of an angelic being has been discovered on a Sumerian stele, a stone column decorated with figures and inscriptions, which archaeologists believe could date back to 4000 BCE. This would date it to 1,000 years after the founding of Sumeria, the world's first civilisation. The stele shows a winged figure, an inhabitant of the seven heavens, pouring the water of life into a king's cup.

The concept of seven heavens inhabited by a hierarchy of celestial beings persists to this day in the teachings of Islam and in the mystical aspect of the Judaeo-Christian traditions, which gave rise to the secular saying, to be 'in seventh heaven', now used to describe exaltation. It therefore seems relatively safe to assume that Sumeria was at least the fount, if not the source, from which these other tributaries sprang and were sustained.

The belief in winged messengers as a celestial species distinct from the gods themselves was disseminated throughout the ancient world with the migration of the Semitic tribes in the 2nd century BCE. In their wake came the itinerant mystics and self-proclaimed prophets, who adopted regional deities to endorse their apocalyptic pronouncements, but in doing so only contributed to the confusion.

It is from the Semitic tradition that we inherited the angels and archangels that are known by name. In the ancient world the celestial messengers of the gods remained anonymous.

## Zoroaster

It was not until the advent of the Persian prophet Zoroaster (*c*.1700–1400 BCE) that angels took on an anthropomorphic form and were given the role of serving a single creator. The prophet is widely believed to have been the first religious leader to preach a monotheistic belief, to envisage angels and demons as opposing forces in an eternal celestial combat, and to have conceived of a Heaven and Hell as places of reward and punishment in terms which subsequently influenced Jewish, Christian and Islamic thought. Through the influence of Zoroastrianism the idea of angels and demons became part of the folklore and religious beliefs of ancient Palestine, which were eventually woven into the fabric of the biblical fables.

## Angels in the Bible

Contrary to popular belief few of the angels mentioned in the

Bible are identified by name. Many of these anonymous messengers either take the form of human beings and are given the designation 'men' (so that the reader isn't quite sure if they really are angels), or are described in a manner which contradicts some of the previous accounts. The fiery seraphim described by Isaiah, for example, bear no relation at all to the unassuming individuals who are said to have appeared before Abraham in the book of Genesis. More significantly, neither type correspond to the benign beings who tens of thousands of ordinary men, women and children claim to have encountered in more recent times.

The angels of both the Old and New Testament are either insubstantial apparitions or creatures so terrifying that they are literally beyond belief. In the New Testament they offer occasional assistance and comfort (Matthew 4:1; Luke 22:43), but their role seems limited to conveying messages. They are described as having little knowledge of the workings of the universe (Matthew 24:36; Peter 1:12), and the only 'fact' we are given is that they are beyond form and gender (Matthew 22:30). It is no wonder that people are tempted to dismiss them outright as the products of fantasy and superstition.

The modern reader could be forgiven for thinking that the anonymous authors of these allegorical tales brought angels on to the stage simply to serve their story, to evoke a sense of wonder, enforce a moral principle or endorse the sanctity of the prophets and patriarchs. In Genesis (18:1), for example, three angels attended Abraham and ate with him in his tent at Mambre, an act that would surely stretch the credulity of even the most ardent believer. None of these heavenly beings, one of which was revealed to be God Himself, possessed wings or halos, and their message was delivered without fanfare or celestial fireworks, but with quiet dignity.

It transpired that God had descended to tell Abraham that his 90-year-old wife Sarah would bear him a son who would father a great nation. Later in the story God would communicate by voice alone, but on this occasion and for no apparent reason He deemed it necessary to appear in person, despite repeated warnings in the Bible that any human who saw God in the flesh would die (Genesis 18:2; Joshua 5:13; Ezekiel 9:2; etc.). At the same time, Abraham tried to persuade the Almightly to spare the cities of Sodom and Gomorrah, which he had heard were designated for destruction. God was adamant, however, that wickedness was to be punished and He sent two baleful angels to murder each and every one of the inhabitants.

We are told that Abraham was visited once more during his lifetime by an angel of the Almighty. On this occasion God demanded that the old man sacrifice his only son, Isaac, the son He had only a few years earlier predicted would father a great nation. Abraham dutifully prepared to carry out what he thought was the will of God, only to be stopped by an angel who assured him that God was only testing him. These episodes, I suggest, reveal more about the cruelty of the times in which the Bible was written, when God was seen by the Hebrews as the ruler of a harsh, unforgiving world, than they do about angels.

Clearly the angel with whom Jacob wrestled (Genesis 32:24) must have been his own conscience rather than a Divine messenger, as the idea of a celestial creature resorting to a physical tussle is absurd, as is the idea of angels having sexual intercourse with human women as described in Genesis (6:2). This is surely pure folklore, a crude attempt to explain how our Divine souls descended into the cold clay of matter. In fact, the angels who consorted with the daughters of men are actually described as 'Sons of God', a common designation in biblical times for any man who considered himself to be devout. It was not a term exclusive to the Hebrews, nor to the founders of Christianity. The Egyptians used the term to denote the Divine origin of their Pharaohs, and the Roman emperors of the East took the title for the same reason.

One gets the impression from these allegorical tales that it is not the characters and the events which we should be focusing on, but the truths and teachings which they conceal. It is my understanding that the key episodes in both the Old and New Testaments, including numerous encounters with angels, were contrived to reveal something of the nature of the invisible realms and the mechanism of creation. (For a more detailed explanation of the spiritual allegory in the Old Testament see my book, *Kabbalah* (Piatkus).)

## The Seven Angels of the Essenes

In biblical times, knowledge of the invisible forces was deemed to be the exclusive preserve of the Hebrew high priests and the various Jewish ascetic sects which flourished throughout Palestine. The most historically significant of these communities were the Essenes and the Nazarenes, of whom Joshua ben Miriam, more commonly known as Jesus, is believed to have been an initiate.

From what we know of the Essenes through their writings contained in the Dead Sea Scrolls, they appear to have practised a form of yoga in which they sought to harmonise the complementary attributes of the Earthly Mother and Heavenly Father within the subtle energy centres of their own body, at points roughly corresponding to the chakras of Eastern philosophy. The sect identified the existence of seven terrestrial 'angels' of the Earthly Mother (the angels of the sun, water, air, earth, life, joy and the Earthly Mother herself), and seven celestial 'angels' of the Heavenly Father (the angels of power, love, wisdom, eternal life, creative work, peace and the Eternal Father), with whom they communed every morning and evening.

It is a reasonable assumption that the Essenes and other pre-Christian esoteric communities were largely responsible for propagating the idea of angels as both the embodiment of natural forces and the personification of personal attributes; an apparent paradox compatible with many Eastern and esoteric traditions which envisage man as a microcosm, a world in miniature. In contrast, the polytheistic civilisations of Egypt and Sumeria and the orthodox religions of revelation (Judaism, Christianity and Islam) envisage angels as discarnate spirits beyond human influence.

## Angels and the Early Church

If the angels of the ancient world and the biblical fables bear little resemblance to the popular image of winged and haloed creatures, or to those described in contemporary accounts of angelic encounters, it is because the benign, beatific things that we envisage today are largely the creation of the Church. The extensive angelologies described by Christian theologians from the early years of the Church and into the modern age are in stark contrast to the fleeting scriptural references found in the New Testament. It would seem that much of Christian angelology is pure supposition and speculation.

From the 1st century CE the nature, purpose and physical appearance of the angelics was the subject of much heated theological debate. In 325 CE the first Ecumenical Council officially accepted the existence of angels and decreed that all good Christians should denounce the pleasures of the physical world and instead aspire to Heaven with the aid of the angelics.

Less than 20 years later a second Council contradicted the first and condemned the worship of angels as an improper act which threatened to interfere with the adoration of Christ. This second Council declared that human beings must consider themselves confined to the flesh through original sin, and as such be beyond the influence of the angels. Confusion continued until 787 CE when the Seventh Ecumenical Synod decided on a compromise, whereby the Church took upon itself what it believed to be the primary role of the angels, to intercede between man and God.

The Synod compounded its misjudgement by endorsing the celestial order proposed by Dionysius the Pseudo-Areopagite, an anonymous Syrian mystic of the 5th century CE who attributed his work to a Greek disciple of the same name. The Greek Dionysius had been converted by St Paul while the Pseudo-Dionysius appears to have been a fraud who not only attempted to pass off his books as the work of his namesake but whose mystical texts must also now be regarded as highly dubious. His *De Hierarchia Celesti* describes a celestial hierarchy of angelic beings who are subservient to the Messiah, and is based on his misunderstanding of several key passages in the New Testament (discussed in Chapter 2).

In adopting his system and taking every element at face value, generations of theologians and numerous self-appointed 'angel experts' of the New Age movement have perpetuated a myth which persists to this day. This 'hierarchy' describes nine orders of angelic beings to which all manner of diverse and contradictory qualities and powers have been attributed over the centuries, all of them, it would seem, erroneous.

## The Medieval Theologians

In the Middle Ages scholar philosophers such as Thomas Aquinas (1225–74) and theologians such as John Duns Scotus (*c*.1265–1308) fashioned the image of the celestials after the vague descriptions to be found in the scriptures and in accordance with the hierarchy described by the Pseudo-Dionysius. Neither man had personal experience to draw upon. Their conclusions are pure supposition, yet they have formed the basis of angel lore for the past 800 years.

Scotus believed that angels were reasoning individuals, made of finer matter than human beings, and that is why they remain invisible to all but those to whom they must impart their message, at which moment they materialise. In contrast, Aquinas was of the opinion that angels were pure intellect who could assume physical form if they wished using mental energy, a theory in keeping with the modern esoteric belief of angels as astral entities – the astral plane being the dimension in which our thoughts are believed to be sufficiently powerful to manipulate the finer astral matter and so create form (see Chapter 4).

## Angel Magic (16th Century)

The rise of Protestant Puritanism in Europe in the early 16th century contributed to a general decline in interest in angels. John Calvin (1509–64 CE), the French theologian who led the Protestant reformation in France and Switzerland, spread a doctrine of predestination which excluded angels from the celestial scheme, although they remained a preoccupation for many Catholic theologians, Jewish mystics and practitioners of the occult. The idea of angels as personifications of natural forces was an assumption that had been made by the magicians of the Renaissance who sought to invoke the angelics as they would other spirits, and command them to obey their will. But the discovery of the New World and the radical, almost revelationary, theories of Galileo (1564–1642 CE) and Copernicus (1473–1543 CE) concerning the nature of the solar system, initiated a public fascination with science at the expense of spiritual matters.

One independent thinker who retained an interest in the celestials was the Elizabethan mathematician and scholar Dr John Dee (1527–1608 CE), astrologer to Queen Mary and Queen Elizabeth I, who claimed to have transcribed the secret and sacred language of the angels through communications with entities in the spirit world. One would have expected Dee's pronouncement to have been dismissed out of hand as the fanciful ravings of an eccentric or charlatan were it not for the fact that the angelic language, which he called 'Enochian' (after the biblical prophet of the same name), stands up to analysis, revealing a credible grammar and syntax of its own. The process of transcription which Dee described in his note-books, now preserved in the British Museum together with his crystal ball, also seems too elaborate to suggest deception.

If his account is to be believed, Dr Dee communicated with the anonymous angelic entity through a medium, Edward Kelley, a dubious character who appears to have deceived his credulous employer in many respects, but not, it would seem, in the matter of the angelic language. In addition to chan-nelling the celestial communications, Kelley convinced Dr Dee that the angels endorsed free love and to that end the doctor should willingly share his wife with the medium!

When he wasn't abusing the good doctor's hospitality Kelley spent hours gazing into a crystal ball in which he claimed to see an angel poring over tablets on which an entire alphabet had been inscribed. These tablets corresponded with a duplicate set in the doctor's possession, although it is not known how he obtained them. As the angel spelt out a word a letter at a time Kelley would call out its position on the tablet, Dr Dee would locate it on his copy and make a note of it. In this tedious fashion Dr Dee took dictation from the angel, one letter at a time, to spell out the words in reverse. Kelley claimed that the angel insisted on this method as the words comprised a set of invocations too powerful to be uttered aloud or even written the correct way round.

If Kelley was practising an elaborate hoax at the doctor's expense he was making it unnecessarily complicated for himself. Of course it could be that Kelley was using the crystal ball as a mirror to read words that he had written on his hands or cuffs, but even if it was possible to read tiny letters in a distorting glass in the half-light, linguists agree that the invention of a pseudo-language of this complexity is a considerable feat of scholarship which would have been beyond someone of Kelley's education and intelligence.

Another possibility is that the pair conspired together to deceive the world, but what would they gain from the deception? Throughout his life Dr Dee was relentlessly hounded by the Church authorities and threatened with prosecution for allegedly practising black magic on the basis of accusations from superstitious members of the public. On one occasion his home was ransacked and his library reduced to ashes by an angry mob. Why should he wish to draw further attention to himself by declaring to be in contact with an angel? Dee enjoyed royal patronage and protection before he met Kelley and gained nothing from their association other than the company of a disingenuous and disagreeable house guest.

A sense of the Enochian language can be gleaned from this typical extract: 'Micma Goho Mad Zir Comselha Zien Biah

Os Londoh Norz Chis Othil Gigipah Vnd-L Chis ta Pu-Im Q Mospleh Teloch [...].', which is said to translate as: 'Behold, saith your God, I am a circle on Whose Hands stand Twelve Kingdoms. Six are the Seats of Living Breath. The rest are as Sharp Sickles or the Horns of Death [...].' This may appear complete gibberish to the uninitiated, but 250 years after his death Dr Dee's diaries were rediscovered and transcribed by S.L. MacGregor Mathers, a founding member of the occult society known as The Hermetic Order of the Golden Dawn. He used it to develop an elaborate and apparently effective system of ceremonial magic which has since been adopted by numerous occult societies and individuals around the world to contact the angels. Even if the claims are entirely false, this must be a unique episode in the history of angelology.

## Emanuel Swedenborg (18th Century)

The movement towards rationalism and reason which swept Europe during the 18th century was known as the Enlightenment, although it was in sharp contrast to the term as understood by the mystics and leaders of the Eastern religions who view enlightenment as an awakening to ultimate truth. This Age of Reason, as it was also known, sneered at anything which could not be proven to be a scientific fact, and as such the subject of angels was seen as a superstitious fancy and not worthy of consideration.

However, as in earlier times, there were those whose own personal experiences defied the dictates of fashion. Emanuel Swedenborg (1688–1772 CE) was a Swedish scientist of considerable repute whose work anticipated the invention of machine guns and submarines. His rational mind and reputation made him a credible witness when he began to describe visions of other realities beyond our physical senses.

Consequently, his claims regarding communications with angels were taken extremely seriously in some quarters.

It was Swedenborg's contention that angels are invisible because they are not made of matter and so cannot reflect the sun's rays. However, he claimed that it is possible to see them by sensitising ourselves to the frequency of vibration on which they exist, a process which involves developing a sixth sense or inner vision. His descriptions of their appearance are convoluted, rather ambiguous and full of allusions to lights and colours of varying hues and intensities.

We are no nearer to knowing what the angels might look like after having read his books, but we can glean something of their nature and of our own from his clairvoyant conversations. For example, the angels told Swedenborg that the soul is not incarcerated in our bodies as an animal in a cage, but is like the water permeating a sponge, simultaneously absorbed in the flesh while remaining in the aura which surrounds us. We are not to see the soul as something limited by form, time or space. God, the angels told him, is Love itself and Heaven a projection of that Love, as are all forms of life, ourselves and the angels included. Hell, on the other hand, is of our own making. As angels are free of the limitations of physical form, and therefore more sensitive to the God-force, they can only express unconditional Love when they appear, whereas we have the free will to either manifest our Divine nature or allow it to be subservient to our animal instincts.

Swedenborg's ideas, particularly those contained in *Angelic Wisdom* and *Heaven and Its Wonders and Hell*, were a profound influence on Goethe, the visionary poet William Blake and another eccentric genius, Rudolph Steiner.

## Rudolph Steiner (19th Century)

Steiner (1861–1925 CE) was an Austrian philosopher who claimed to have clairvoyant communications with celestial beings, namely nature spirits and angels, from the age of eight. As with Swedenborg, his expertise in the sciences (mathematics and medicine) and his prodigious talents in the arts (in which he excelled as a sculptor, painter and architect) lent credibility to his extraordinary claims.

One of his central ideas was that we are all guided by a guardian angel whose influence is strongest during childhood and old age, but who draws back during adulthood to allow us to develop our personalities through experience.

Despite his incredible intellect and perceptive powers, Steiner clung on to the dubious hierarchy of angels proposed by Dionysius and he even added further beings from Greek and Judaic sources to make a full and impressive complement of celestial creatures. But he made an interesting distinction between angels, archangels and a more evolved group which he called the archai. The former, he believed, were water spirits (astral entities whose world is traditionally symbolised by water), their sphere of influence extending to individual human beings. Archangels are fire spirits (inhabitants of the higher world of creation whose symbol is fire), who influence the evolution of the group-soul, that is a race of people. Above these he envisaged the archai, great universal spirits who oversee the progress of the human species and from whom descend the enlightened souls – the prophets, teachers, saints and Bodhisattvas of each age.

Steiner's conclusions reveal the calculated detachment of an intellectual, rather than the compassion and ecstasy of a genuine mystic, but they have nevertheless enriched and permeated angelology to this day.

## *The New Age*

The proliferation of angel workshops, meditation tapes and books which currently vie for attention in almost every country in the world are proof that our fascination with angels persists even into the age of routine space flight and genetic engineering. And yet, we seem no nearer to understanding the nature of these beings than were our ancestors.

One aspect of modern angelology is, however, unique to the present, and that is the idea that the veil separating our world from the angelics is becoming more translucent year upon year as our awareness of other realities increases. Even if we are only reading about spiritual matters or meditating for the purpose of self-development we are contributing as individuals towards a global raising of consciousness. The angels are, of course, aware of this development, and so they draw nearer to entrust us with more and more knowledge, creating a spiralling upsurge of energy to take us towards the next stage of our evolution.

The workshops, tapes and books may differ in detail, but all seem to be in agreement that angelic encounters are more numerous now than ever before. More significantly, they all convey a common message which the angels are bringing at this crucial moment in our history, a message that is not limited to endorsements of religious figures or doctrines, but a general communication to humanity from those who oversee evolution. It says that we too are Divine beings with the capacity to love unconditionally and without exception; our future on this planet is dependent upon our willingness to manifest our Divine nature, to see the Divine in all things, to love as they do, unconditionally and with every atom of our being.

# 2

# Hierarchy and Cosmology

Angels are spirits, but it is not because they are spirit that they are angels. They become angels when they are sent. For the name and angel refers to their office, not their nature. You ask the name of this nature, it is spirit; you ask its office, it is that of an Angel, which is a messenger.

Saint Augustine

## The Myth of the Thrones, Dominions, Principalities and Powers

In the early years of the Church new converts to Christianity found themselves under pressure to renounce their faith. For this reason evangelists, such as St Paul, took it upon themselves to send 'circulars' to these communities in the hope of stiffening their resolve.

In St Paul's letters to the Ephesians, the Romans and a sect at Colossos (whose authenticity is hotly disputed by scholars), this zealous convert urges the new disciples to strengthen their resolve against their persecutors and envisage themselves as ultimately triumphant. God, he reminds them, is on their side. 'For by God were all things created that are in Heaven, and that are in earth, visible and invisible, whether they be thrones or dominions, or principalities, or powers: all things were created by Him and for Him' (Col. 1:16).

It is surely only a matter of common sense to see that the thrones, dominions, principalities and powers to which he refers are not individual ranks in an angelic hierarchy, as some suppose, but symbols of temporal power which exist under the Will of God. It was Paul's intention to show the new converts that the laws decreed by earthly rulers must always accord with the universal laws and the laws of nature which are expressions of God.

The word 'thrones' evokes an image of a succession of kings and queens whose power is fleeting and whose grandeur ultimately turns to dust. A 'dominion' traditionally refers to a land governed by a single ruler or an elected body, while a 'principality' derives its name from the fact that it is ruled by a prince, or a territory from which a prince draws his title. That being so, 'powers' would cover the remainder, such as self-administering states or other centres of civilisation invested with authority and influence. Paul is therefore clearly listing terrestrial authorities in order of descent. There is no reference in the passage to angels and no reason to assume, as so many have done, that he is describing angels, their status or their duties.

There is no hierarchy of angels, but the topography and inhabitants of the physical world are a reflection of the celestial realms. Ranking living beings in order of merit, achievement or capability is a human concept.

The contrast between terrestrial and celestial power is even clearer in a subsequent passage. 'Far above all principality, and power, and might, and dominion, and every name that is named, not only in this world, but also in that which is to come [is God]' (Eph. 1:21). And again, in a later letter he makes a distinction between angels and the temporal symbols of power. 'For I am persuaded that neither death, nor life, nor angels, nor principalities, nor powers, nor things present, nor things to come; nor height, nor depth, nor any other creature, shall be able to separate us from the love of God' (Rom. 8:35–39).

If we dismiss the thrones, dominions, principalities and powers for the reasons stated, there are still five ranks of angels to be accounted for. These filtered into the Christian consciousness through various sources and were identified in medieval angelology as the seraphim, cherubim, virtues, archangels and angels.

I suggest that the virtues, a genus of angel whose origins are unknown but whose name derives from the Latin *virtus* meaning manliness, are simply the cardinal virtues of prudence, justice, fortitude and temperance personified by early theologians as the Divine attributes latent in man. As such they would be qualities to aspire to which the medieval mind would have symbolised in a celestial ideal – an angel – as a representation of our potential divinity.

This leaves just four angelic hosts whose existence may well have some basis in fact, but whose nature, purpose and place in creation have been confused by superstition and a literal reading of scripture.

## Seraphim

The first and only recorded description of the seraphim in the Bible appears in the Old Testament (Isaiah 6), where the prophet is blessed with a vision of six-winged seraphim standing around the throne of God and singing His praises. The fact that the seraphim merit only one mention in the Bible suggests that the name does not denote a specific species of angelic being, but instead identifies a characteristic or quality which the prophet saw in these formless supernatural beings.

The Hebrew noun *sarap*, from which the name is derived, simply means 'fiery', so that Isaiah might have been describing a being of light, of intense brilliance, rather than a particular creature distinct from the other angels. This would also explain why the seraphim are not referred to elsewhere; it was the word Isaiah chose to *describe* an angel rather than the name of an angel. Imagine a situation in which two people might see what they think is a UFO but describe it as being alternately 'bright' and 'shiny'. If their descriptions of the supposed sighting are unearthed and translated 2,000 years later when language will have altered beyond our recognition, it might be thought that the witnesses saw two different species of alien life, one being 'bright' and the other 'shiny'.

Isaiah describes one of these fiery beings breaking off in mid-chorus to pick a burning coal from the temple altar with a pair of tongs, then dropping it into his mouth to purify his lips and purge him of sin. If it is *not* to be taken literally, it could be a symbolic description of a profound spiritual experience for which conventional language would be inadequate; otherwise it would serve no purpose at all and the text would not have survived the numerous translations and revisions which have taken place over the centuries.

So, we can assume that the throne and the winged being of light are significant, but of what?

## Ezekiel and the Four Winged Creatures

Isaiah's description of God seated on a throne surrounded by the celestials invites comparison with the vision of Ezekiel.

The traditional interpretation of the vision in which Ezekiel described a fiery chariot drawn by four winged creatures each with four faces, is that the figure is representative of God and the whole symbolic of the apocalypse to come at the end of the world. In contrast, the Jewish mystic, or Kabbalist, understands that the vision is a revelation of a greater reality, the various elements symbolising the structure of existence.

The structure of existence envisaged by the Kabbalist is a Divine scheme whose validity has been tested through personal revelation and experience by each initiate over the centuries. However, it is not necessary for those wishing to work with angels to subscribe to the Kabbalah, only to understand its basic principles, as these form the basis of the Western esoteric tradition and of much angelic work.

In the Kabbalistic scheme the figure seated on the throne is symbolic of primordial man, who was created in the likeness of God and who exists in the highest of four worlds, the World of Emanation, the realm of unity and perfection. The throne represents the World of Creation, the next level in order of descent from the Divine, which can be considered as the dimension of spirit. The chariot symbolises the lower World of Formation, or the astral plane, with Ezekiel himself representing man in the fourth world, the World of Action, which is our physical world. The four winged creatures represent the four realms within each world, for the Kabbalah presents a picture of ever unfolding creation, of worlds within worlds, and their four faces the corresponding elements of fire, air, water and earth at work within these.

It is the work of the Kabbalist to experience and understand the interplay between the Divine attributes at each of these levels, and to manifest these in themselves. By doing so we can each realise the image of the perfect human being who is a reflection of God.

## Cherubim

In contrast to the seraphim, the hybrid, multi-faceted cherubim appear nearly 100 times in the course of the Old Testament, as if to emphasise the significance of what they represent. They are described as having eagle's wings, a human face, the body of a lion and the features of a bull. The very same symbolic imagery occurs in Ezekiel's vision; the human face is said by the Kabbalists to be symbolic of Divine man in the World of Emanation; the element of fire, the eagle's wings, are believed to be symbolic of the World of Creation; the element of air, the lion's body, represents the World of Formation; and the element of water, the bull's features, corresponds to the World of Action and the element of earth.

The contrast in image with the cherubim of the Christian angelic hierarchy, and with the cherubic babies beloved of Renaissance artists, suggests that the name has again been misappropriated to describe a species of angel, with little consideration for what the word originally denoted – a symbol of the invisible forces.

## Angels and Archangels

Angels and archangels are therefore left to populate the celestial realms, a proposition which appears to be confirmed by the esoteric (hidden) teachings of the Old Testament. In the book of Genesis, the creation of the 'fowl of the air' is believed to be a reference to the emergence of the archangels in the World of Creation (the realm of pure spirit symbolised by the element of air), while the creation of the 'fish of the sea' is understood to refer to the emergence of the angels in the World of Formation (the astral realm whose symbol is water). According to Kabbalistic tradition the remaining worlds are devoid of angelics, the World of Emanation being the realm of the Divine essence and the World of Action being our own physical dimension.

While we remain in the physical body we cannot possibly differentiate between such mutable amorphous forms or understand exactly what it is that we are experiencing. The number of angelic encounters throughout history should be proof enough that angels and archangels exist, but they would appear to be formless beings of light and pure consciousness, which only assume a form so that we can relate to them as entities. To rank them like soldiers and give them generic titles as if they were a readily identifiable species of exotic animal life is plainly absurd.

We like to think of angels as eternal and unchanging because it satisfies our desire for stability. However, angels cannot possibly be inert, limited to one stage of evolution, or ranked in a static hierarchy, when everything else in creation is continually evolving, striving consciously or instinctively towards its ultimate potential. Even single-cell creatures divide and evolve towards a higher form of life, and plants strive towards the light even when the seed or bulb has been planted with its roots to the surface. As human beings we are continually searching for a meaning and purpose to life and through that soul-searching we develop greater self-awareness and knowledge of the world about us. Why then would angels, who are traditionally envisaged as being closer to the Divine than human beings, be denied the same opportunity to evolve? Perhaps the question we need to ask is not: 'do angels exist?', but rather: 'is it our limited perception and understanding that is obscuring them from our sight'?

Mary Baker Eddy in *Science and Health* said that angels are not etherealised human beings. She believes human conjecture confers upon angels its own forms of thought, marked by superstition which suggests creatures that are winged; but this is only fancy. She continues by saying that our concept of angels has behind it no more reality than the sculptor's thought when he carves a statue which embodies his conception of an unseen quality or condition such as freedom.

## Our Divine Destiny?

One of the most intriguing and unusual visions of the celestial hierarchy and what might lie beyond it was claimed to have been obtained during a past-life regression session by angelic researcher and author Sophy Burnham. In *A Book of Angels*, her semi-autobiographical account of a life illuminated by supernatural encounters, Sophy stresses that she remains sceptical about the regression process and accepts that her experience is highly subjective. But for me it has a ring of truth. I have personally undergone past-life regression therapy on several occasions and have had many other visionary experiences which lead me to regard her experience with less scepticism than she does.

Like Professor Harlow, whose vision is recounted in Chapter 3, Sophy is a pragmatist whose academic background instilled in her the need to question and prove the truth of everything before she could accept it as fact. When she agreed to submit to a past-life regression session she did not believe in reincarnation and was ready to dismiss all inner visions as the product of an overactive imagination; in many ways she was the ideal person to test the validity of the process.

She was put into a relaxed, meditative state by her friend and therapist, and having obtained a sense of stillness and detachment she was guided through a number of past-life memories. Details of her journey were obtained by asking her to describe what she could see and recording the results for later transcription.

After her friend had led her through a number of previous lives he asked if she wanted to view a future life to which she eagerly agreed. She soon found herself among a cloudy brown haze floating free of her body. When asked to look down at her feet and describe what she was wearing she dissolved into giggles, feeling that the very concept of a physical body was absurd. She was apparently in the spirit, free of physical form and able to fly in any direction and manner at will. She describes it as an exhilarating sensation.

When asked if she had wings she thought the idea ridiculous, but with the thought manifested a pair of wings to please her questioner, and she remembers thinking how awkward and unnecessary these were given her ability to move fluidly through timeless space. Her mood changed when asked to stop flitting about and put her feet on the ground, as she became panicky, afraid that she would crush the people on the earth for she now realised that she was enormous, the essence of her being stretching across the sky. Then she intuitively recalled how to contain her discarnate form by concentrating her energy so that she could move among humans while remaining invisible to them. But the sense of being confined to the physical world again struck her as ludicrous and she gave way to another fit of giggles.

Observing human beings scurrying about, preoccupied with the minutiae of their lives, unable to focus on anything for very long and getting worked up about insignificant matters, seemed so senseless to her, and yet she found them endearing. It seemed to her that they actually enjoyed the sensation of fear or loss, perhaps because that is what made them feel alive. Or perhaps it was because their senses were so dulled by being confined to the flesh that it took such frissons to stimulate them.

At this point in the session it appears that Sophy became aware that she was a 'Young One', not yet fully in control of her powers, who would later be assigned to watch over these human beings and wait upon their call for help. But until they requested her help she knew that she would not be permitted to intervene. Her friend asked if there were others like her and she replied that there were 'Big Ones' (the archangels perhaps?) in the middle distance, but that she was apprehensive about joining them because she felt intimidated by their superiority. To join them she had to become one of them, that was the law, each to their own place and purpose. As she drew near to the 'Big Ones' her playfulness was replaced by a stillness and serenity. Before she could reach these beings, however, she was asked to go to the next stage to describe what her friend called the 'Sages'.

In becoming one of these beings she was aware that she no longer had form, nor the means of describing this higher state of being. Her friend's questions were meaningless, for in this state of exquisite nothingness there was no distinction between gender or self – the very concept of being was beyond human understanding. She sensed that she existed at a level where she was 'absorbed in harmony, the humming of pure love'. The work of the 'Sage', or the 'Compassionate' as she called this being, was to emit the vibration on which the universe subsists. The answers she might be able to give were of no importance; what was important was the love transmitted in that silent, emanating sound.

Asked if she was God she responded in the negative, but only because she was not what a human understands by the word. Her understanding was that it was all much more complex than the question of a single God. God is the centre of what it created but also outside it; God is the source which had no beginning and will never end; God-ness is in all of us whose ultimate task is to release the silent sound of compassion for compassion is God. Beyond the state of the Sage is the void, into which its formlessness must be absorbed.

## EXERCISE: ENTERING THE ANGELIC WORLD

The following exercise is designed to give you a sense of the unity of existence and your place in it. It can be done either sitting down or lying flat on a bed or mat.

☆ When you have made yourself comfortable, begin by focusing on breathing in a rhythm of four-two-four. Count up to four as you slowly inhale, holding the breath for a count of two, and count again for four as you exhale, pausing for a count of two before inhaling again. Repeat this cycle until you feel sufficiently relaxed and peaceful. Counting your breathing in this way will establish a good rhythm for meditation and at the same time still the restless mind.

☆ As you focus on your breathing, become aware that this is the gaseous or airy element of your body. Next focus your attention on the blood in your veins, circulating throughout your system and maintaining the vital organs. This is the watery element. Then feel the weight and density of your body with the bones that serve as the supporting structure and the flesh that gives you form. This is the earth element of your body. Finally, focus on the heat in your skin and imagine energy radiating outwards in an aura of white and gold light, with you feeling still and serene at the centre. This is the fire element.

☆ Now move your attention to the outer world where mountains strain upwards towards the sky and try to imagine the force which fashioned them from molten rock millions of years ago. Know that this molten matter is bubbling and churning in the depths of the earth under your feet at this moment. It has done so for aeons and will continue to do so long after you have gone from this place. This is the fire element of the earth.

☆ Now return through the layers of rock that mark the millennia, past the multi-coloured minerals and crystals to the surface of the planet where tides ebb and flow under the influence of the moon, where waves crash upon the shore, and where, further inland, waterfalls cascade in foaming torrents of clear, fresh, mountain water and streams trickle from the hills to the lowlands to refresh the fields. Here the reservoirs and lakes are becalmed like vast burnished mirrors reflecting the clouds which will replenish them. The earth, too, depends for its survival on the element of water.

☆ Now see a breeze ruffle leaves on the shoreline and send a ripple across the surface of the water. Watch with detachment as the wind picks up strength, scattering seeds from plants and trees across the fields and carrying clouds across the seas. Over the centuries the wind has reduced mountains to grains of soil, but it has also been harnessed to carry explorers and merchants across the oceans to establish great civilisations in new lands. The element of air is vital to the lifecycle of the world.

☆ Now rise up through the clouds, look down on the earth from the deep silence of space and sense the earth breathing, evolving and revitalising itself from the energy of the sun just as you do. Know that the earth and all life which exists upon the planet are interdependent elements of the same universal life force, the same evolutionary impulse.

☆ Now rise higher through the blackness of space towards a single star which seems to expand and intensify in brilliance as you approach, until you see that it is not a star at all but a spiral of living light, a seemingly endless tunnel composed of celestial beings in angelic form. As you are drawn up through this tunnel of light you have a sense of coming home, a sense of the inseparable nature of all things, and of overwhelming, unconditional love which welcomes you as a vital spark in this eternal source of light.

☆ Rise higher through this angelic realm to the inner universe of the archangels who dwell in a stillness and harmony of being beyond human comprehension. Abide a while in their company and when you feel ready to return, ask for the blessing of their loving presence in your life and for their guidance from this moment on.

☆ Now descend back into the angelic realm and drift down gently through the spiral of light into the realm of time and space. Return to our solar system, hover over planet earth and then descend through the clouds. Skim over the seas, the coast, the fields and follow the road that leads to your home. Become aware once again of your surroundings, the weight of your body, your breath, and when you are ready, open your eyes.

# 3

# Ghosts, Guides and Guardian Angels

Another question regularly asked during my classes and workshops is whether angels are the same beings as guides or even ghosts. I will make this distinction as clear as possible from the outset, and by doing so will hopefully take some of the fear or anxiety out of making contact with higher discarnate beings.

## Ghosts

It is my understanding that there are two categories of ghosts. The first are simply echoes of people who have died and left an impression with the violence of their passing, or through their strong emotional bond with a particular place. The second type are the restless spirits of the dead.

The former are harmless, in that there is no consciousness to contend with. The departing spirit has moved on to another dimension leaving its image imprinted in the ether through the strength of its emotional ties with a place or person associated with that place. That is why these 'ghosts' do not respond to, or acknowledge, the presence of the living.

In contrast, the restless, discarnate spirits of the dead are potentially more dangerous in that they are often emotionally disturbed, fettered to the physical world to which they no longer belong. It could be that these are 'harmless' individuals who are simply not aware that they are dead, either because in life they could not imagine an existence other than the physical, or because they are bound by habit to carry out the routine, mundane tasks with which they filled their lives. These spirits are constantly urged by the angels to awaken from their sleepwalking state to their new reality by being shown that they have no influence on the physical world – whatever chores they do are never completed, for example. In time they will awaken from their dream of life and leave for the higher realms under the guidance of the angels.

Other restless spirits might be distressed to find themselves wandering aimlessly in their familiar environment without the ability to affect anything on the physical plane or communicate with the living. But again, they are never left to suffer for long, as a primary task of the angels is to smooth the process of the human spirit between the worlds. They also help those who have bound themselves to our world through negative emotions such as hate, fear and jealousy, or through addiction to drink or drugs, although the latter usually find themselves wandering in a hell of their own making, a borderland between the worlds. Because of the strength of the emotions involved, the angels are often not able to make a sufficient impression on these people, who need to forgive those they feel have wronged them and let go of their attachments.

## Guides

Occasionally, loved ones who have passed over can come back to give us guidance, reassurance, to convey a specific message or simply to say goodbye. These are not guides as such, but materialisations of a living spirit whose desire to communicate has been so strong that it has enabled it to temporarily cross the veil between the worlds. In contrast, a guide is a spirit who having passed over then decides to return periodically (often over a long period – even an entire lifetime), to help a specific individual for whom it feels an affinity, or with whom it has had a relationship in a previous life. We are all said to have at least one, sometimes two guides at any one point in our lives, and these leave us at key phases in our development to allow others to take over who are more suitable to guide us through the next stage of life.

A guide will never impose itself upon someone who does not wish to work with it or be guided by it, but will always respect the will of the individual to whom it has been assigned or attracted. If it senses that the living person is fearful of the unknown its initial approaches may be limited to bringing what might otherwise be seen as good luck into that individual's life, but in such a contrived manner that it should be obvious to the person that they are receiving help from beyond. It might then project its image or thoughts into the unconscious of the chosen individual, establishing contact in their dreams or during meditations. From there it might make its presence felt through physical sensations, such as stroking the person's face, which will feel like the brush of a cobweb against the skin, before finally appearing at an opportune moment if it deems it necessary.

Some people who work with angels and guides have never actually seen their invisible helpers, but claim to have an

41

acute sense of their presence and are content with that. One reason for this might be that unconsciously they know that these are beings of light who only assume a recognisable form for our benefit, and therefore a manifestation would serve no purpose.

Both ghosts and guides invariably assume the form they took for their last incarnation on earth (although a loved one sometimes appears older or younger than we remember them), but an angel is a discarnate entity and will only assume a physical form temporarily to put us at our ease or to control a physical object such as a car that is out of control. An important thing to bear in mind is that a psychic, or a sensitive as many now prefer to be called, can often 'see' guides or the ghosts of loved ones who are trying to communicate with the living, but very few can differentiate between what appear to be guides and other images which could be lingering impressions of a client's past life. So, if you are told by a psychic that they can see a native American chief or a Chinaman standing beside you (two common forms assumed by spirit guides), these might instead be aspects of your own personality which come to the surface whenever your interest in spiritual matters is aroused.

## Guardian Angels

Although angels have assumed many forms throughout the centuries, often conforming to the expectations of the person to whom they appear, they are quite distinctive from guides or ghosts. While guides and ghosts are frequently described as being transparent and conveying a feeling of unease, even if their mission is a benevolent one, angels appear as radiant, incandescent beings of light and colour whose presence brings warmth and an overwhelming sense of peace and well-being.

Few descriptions of an angel are ever exactly alike. Even when the same angel is said to have been seen by two or more witnesses, such as those reputedly seen at the Battle of Mons (see below), the descriptions can differ so enormously that one is tempted either to dismiss the visions outright as figments of the imagination, or to accept them as impressions of a subjective spiritual experience.

For example, the 14th-century French St Francisca described her guardian angel as having long curly blond hair and a face 'whiter than snow, redder than the blush rose'. His full-length robes would alter in colour from one materialisation to the next, but even when he chose to remain invisible she could sense his presence. When he materialised Francisca claimed that his radiance was so bright that she could read her night-time prayers in the light that he cast. However, when her spiritual adviser and confessor announced that he too could see her angel he described it as having the appearance of a young child.

Perhaps, ultimately, we are left with Meister Eckhart's definition of an angel as being simply 'an idea of God'. And as we all know, everyone has their own idea of what God might be, an idea which is constantly altering as we grow and evolve.

## The Angels of Mons

One of the most unusual celestial sightings occurred during the First World War. It was unusual, and perhaps even unique in the annals of angelic encounters, because the vision was reputedly witnessed by dozens of soldiers and apparently substantiated independently by numerous non-combatants.

The initial reports were based on rumours which had begun in the field hospitals behind the lines after the Battle of Mons in August 1914, when nurses reported hearing wounded French and British soldiers tell of an army of angels coming to their aid during the allied retreat. Those who were dying told of what they had seen with a serenity and elation that the nurses could not readily account for other than by believing that the men had indeed shared a spiritual vision. One soldier claimed to have seen 'a strange light' above the German front line which had a distinct outline and which he was adamant was not a reflection of the moon. As he gazed in awe, three celestial beings dressed in long, flowing garments of gold emerged from the light, and at the very moment that the middle figure spread his wings the German advance slowed, allowing the allies to escape. Others spoke of seeing an angel with luminous wings whose appearance seemed to impede their German pursuers.

Remarkably, many French soldiers shared a similar vision, although some of them identified the figure as the Archangel Michael, while the more patriotic thought the vision was of St Joan. The British tended to interpret what they had seen as the personification of the spirit of St George, the patron saint of England. Despite these variations in interpretation, many at least agreed on the details, describing a mounted knight with yellow hair clad in golden armour and brandishing a sword.

A curious postscript to this encounter is that the German regiment in question also claimed to have seen something supernatural and to have been rendered powerless to pursue the fleeing troops. When reprimanded by their officers the German soldiers claimed that something had startled their horses and sent them bolting back to their own lines. When they looked towards what were in fact a scattering of ragged, retreating troops they were convinced that instead they saw thousands of armed men holding the allied front line.

The legend of the Angels of Mons, as it became known, was confused in the public mind when it became known that the English writer Arthur Machen had published a short story on a similar theme in the *London Evening News* three weeks after the battle. Machen's story described how an army of ghostly English bowmen from the time of Agincourt had come to the rescue of the retreating forces. It was a work of fiction inspired by patriotic accounts that Machen had read of a brave, orderly retreat, and was not a response to the rumours about angels of which he claimed to have been unaware at the time. But Machen was convinced that his story had started the rumours and he expended considerable effort attempting to assure the public that the Angels of Mons were a product of mass hysteria brought on by shell-shock and battle fatigue.

## Angelic Intervention

I am often asked why angels sometimes intervene when they have not been called, and occasionally refuse to intervene when someone has appealed to them for help. It is my understanding that we have all chosen to incarnate on earth to learn whatever we need to learn in order to evolve and to take certain experiences back to the Higher Self and the group-soul. If we knew that all our distress calls would be answered and resolved by Divine intervention, we would not take the risks or decisions in life that are necessary to learn those particular lessons, painful though they might be.

All indications suggest that angels are highly evolved beings, but the human will galvanised with the power of our emotions can blind and deafen us to the quiet inner voices of those who have our best interests at heart. It is one of the universal laws that humans have the right to exercise free will in all matters concerning their own lives, and that the angels will not intervene unless called upon by us to do so, or unless the circumstances are extreme, if we were to threaten the life of another person, for example. Sometimes not even such extremes would prompt intervention however, as the laws of karma take precedence where a difficult relationship between people might have been set up to help resolve a conflict carried over from a previous life and bring everything back into balance between them.

In cases where a restless and malevolent spirit will not depart in peace it may be necessary for the living person who is being victimised, so to speak, or a third party who is concerned for their well-being, to enlist the help of the angels. The angels are then free to intervene because someone has exercised their free will and called upon them. It does not matter that it is not the restless spirit themselves, nor even their 'victim', who has called out to them. But be assured, such instances are not as common as the media and the movies would have you believe. They are extremely rare, so don't worry unduly. Besides, another universal law states that 'like attracts like', which means that if you want to work with angels and guides for the highest good of all concerned and without any selfish motive, then you will attract only the Divine powers and become stronger and more self-aware in the process.

## Angelic Companions

According to some accounts, angels may not feel it necessary to materialise if their charges are not in physical danger, but will instead make their presence felt to bring reassurance and comfort in difficult times. On one occasion the celebrated British polar explorer, Sir Ernest Henry Shackleton, who commanded three expeditions to the Antarctic, reported the presence of an invisible companion whose company helped to see him through a particularly arduous stage of his journey.

Mountaineer Francis Sydney Smythe had a similar experience during his solo ascent of Mount Everest in 1933. He later described the profound effect that the benign presence had on him by saying that whenever it drew close he sensed that he could not come to any harm. So real was this feeling of being shadowed by another being that on one occasion Smythe instinctively divided his provisions in two with the intent of offering one portion to his 'companion'. His rational mind won through, however, prompting him to dismiss the episode as an hallucination attributable to stress, solitude, high altitude and exhaustion, although imagination could not account for the feeling of being protected.

## An Angelic Materialisation

Of course there are other more rational explanations for these encounters, including the idea that angelic assistants might be a projection from the witnesses' own unconscious triggered by extreme fatigue or stress. Because they originate from within, the contention is that these illusions, if that is what they are, will invariably take the form and face of the witness themselves, a phenomenon which has given rise to the myth of the 'doppelganger' (German for 'double walker' or 'shadow').

An intriguing example of this type of encounter has been described by an American soldier, Gordon Barrows. On a bitterly cold night in 1946 Barrows was so eager to get home after having been discharged from the US Army that he drove non-stop for 18 hours across the most inhospitable desert terrain in Wyoming. By the time he reached the outskirts of Laramie he had pushed himself to the point of exhaustion and was in danger of falling asleep at the wheel. At that critical moment he noticed a lone hitchhiker in the road ahead and pulled over. But as Barrows wound the window down to offer the stranger a lift he had the fright of his life. The hitch-hiker was his exact double. The only distinguishing factor was the man's clothes; the hitchhiker wore light army denims despite the sub-zero temperatures which would have disabled any normal human being. Yet the man did not appear to be suffering any ill effects from the biting cold.

Barrows was so exhausted by this time that it didn't strike him as odd. When the stranger offered to take the wheel the ex-soldier was too relieved to resist and slid over to the passenger seat where he soon fell asleep. He awoke some hours later to find his companion sitting silent and motionless at the wheel of the car which had come to a stop on a clear stretch of road. Barrows had barely time to thank him before the stranger climbed out of the car and disappeared into the desert. Since that night Barrows has been convinced that he would have frozen to death in the desert had he not been helped by his own 'spirit double'. The encounter has been cited in several medical text books as a typical 'doppelganger hallucination', or autoscopy, to use its technical term. And yet the clinical definition of the phenomenon only allows for a partial apparition, never the full figure, which does not conform to Barrows' experience.

The clinical definition describes the apparition as being a life-sized mirror image of a living person, invariably of a ghostly transparency, and often in monochrome or 'washed-out' colours. They do not appear solid and convincingly life-like nor act independently as Barrows' 'double' is said to have done, but replicate the movement and expressions of their physical counterpart as if they were a reflection. So, if it was not a psychological phenomenon it must have been a physical being which took control of the car, which strongly suggests the rarest form of angelic encounter – a materialisation.

## The Professor's Tale

Almost all angelic encounters on record describe how angels have intervened to save people from physical danger or rescued them from the depths of despair. But it seems that they can also affect our lives in more subtle ways, as the experience of Professor S. Ralph Harlow of Massachusetts illustrates. Professor Harlow's encounter, which occurred in the 1930s and was widely reported in esoteric magazines across the USA, adds considerable weight to the case for the existence of angels. For one, the professor was a respected academic with an MA from Columbia University, a BA from Harvard and a PhD from Hartford Theological Seminary. He was frequently called to testify in legal cases as a reliable and honest witness, and he considered himself to be a rationalist who believed little that had not been proven by scientific investigation. The second significant factor is that his story was corroborated by another witness, his wife Marion.

In his account the professor recalls that he and Marion were walking in the woods on a crisp, bright day in early spring when they heard muted voices behind them. The voices appeared to be coming closer, but when the couple turned to see who was approaching, no-one was there. It was then that they sensed that the voices were not only behind them, but also above them. Illogical though it seemed, they both instinctively looked upwards and were startled but exhilarated to see a group of what they later described as 'glorious, beautiful creatures that glowed with spiritual beauty' floating overhead at a height of about ten feet. 'There were six of them,' the professor remembered, 'young beautiful women dressed in flowing white garments and engaged in earnest conversation. If they were aware of our existence they gave no indication of it. Their faces were perfectly clear to us [...]'

Neither the professor nor his wife could understand what the celestial beings were saying to each other although they were clearly audible. Professor Harlow likened it to listening to a group of people talking outside a house with the windows and doors shut. 'They seemed to float past us, and their graceful motion seemed natural – as gentle and peaceful as the morning itself. As they passed, their conversation grew fainter and fainter until it faded out entirely [...] It would be an understatement to say that we were astounded.' Being a trained observer the professor's first reaction was to ask his wife to describe exactly what she had seen and heard so that he could be sure that he had not imagined it. Incredibly, her description was identical in every respect to what he too had witnessed.

Nevertheless, whenever he told the story he felt the need to justify himself by adding that he had told it with the same faithfulness and respect for truth and accuracy as he would tell it on the witness stand. 'Perhaps I can claim no more for it than that it has had a deep effect on our own lives. For this experience [...] greatly altered our thinking.'

## The Angelic Teacher

Although we tend to think of angels in terms of non-corporeal beings of light whose appearances are almost manifestations of faith, if we instead consider the original definition of angels as primarily Divine messengers, we might find that each and every one of us has been blessed with an angelic encounter at least once in our lives. The following story, told to me by one of my pupils, serves as an example of how the Divine uses highly evolved souls as messengers and guides.

The lady in question, whom I shall call Mary for the sake of the story, attended one of my angel workshops and was keen to develop her natural psychic abilities. The course that she joined after leaving mine was unsatisfactory, however, and she was feeling frustrated. She asked the angels for help and guidance and now believes that she received it in a very curious and special way. The next time she attended her psychic awareness class she found herself alone with the teacher and one other pupil. For various reasons the rest of the class had decided to skip that particular meeting, but not because they too were frustrated with the course, as they all returned the following week. That was the first curious element.

Mary was introduced to the other pupil who was new to the course. He was a man in his early forties with steel grey hair and piercing blue-grey eyes, but his most striking feature was his stature. He was an unusually large man, not fat, or even stocky, more of a gentle giant, and he spoke and moved in an uncommonly graceful manner. When he handled a pack of Tarot cards he seemed to be almost stroking the pictures as if attuning himself to the subtle frequency which they symbolised, and as he was doing so Mary noticed that his fingers were extraordinarily long, perhaps 14 or 15 centimetres.

The teacher was as ineffectual and disorganised as usual which seemed to give the man the cue he was waiting for, and he took over the evening and taught Mary what she wanted to know about reading the Tarot, developing her intuition and practising telepathy. He answered her questions to her satisfaction, including those she hadn't yet put into words, and during one particular exercise he not only told her the name of the card that she was holding, but also the card she had been thinking of while she had been shuffling the deck.

He had been introduced to her as Peter and happened to mention that he was working in the building trade, which struck Mary as unusual as her husband was in the same line of work and had always said that everyone in that profession seems to have their name truncated, in which case he would have introduced himself as Pete. It was an almost insignificant detail, but it has nagged at her ever since. There was something deeply reassuring and yet otherworldly about him.

His innate dignity seemed to pervade the room, and at one point the teacher's young daughter came down to complain to her mother that she couldn't sleep because there was something in the house which was making her restless. When the little girl saw Peter she was transfixed, and later admitted that she was hoping he would pick her up and kiss her although she is normally very wary of strangers and not a particularly affectionate child. When Peter left the house he seemed to sense the little girl's thoughts and bent down and pecked her on the cheek. When Mary followed him just a moment later he was nowhere to be seen.

'It was impossible for a man of that size to just disappear,' she told me in disbelief. 'It was a wide road clear of cars in both directions and with no other buildings or side roads into which he could have gone. Even if he had run off or jumped into his car and raced down the road, I was only a matter of seconds behind him and would have seen him leaving. I'm absolutely convinced that he had been sent to restore my faith in the spiritual path and to teach me what I needed to know at that point in my life. I am not a highly imaginative or fanciful person, but there is no doubt in my mind that he was an angel.'

*Be not afraid to have strangers in your house, for some thereby have entertained angels unawares.*

Hebrews (13:2)

The following exercise helps to increase awareness of when and how the angels have intervened in your life and for what purpose. Reviewing your life as a continual interaction between yourself and the celestial powers in this way will strengthen the connection between you and your invisible protectors.

## EXERCISE: HALL OF LIFE

☆ Make yourself comfortable with your back straight, your feet flat on the floor and slightly apart, and your hands on your thighs. Close your eyes and begin to focus on your breathing. Take slow, deep, regular breaths. Expel the tension with every out-breath. When you inhale, breathe in a golden light which warms and calms you. Feel yourself relaxing with every breath.

☆ Imagine that it is night and you are alone outside in a strangely familiar landscape. It is a place of peace. Take the first impression that comes into your mind and do not try to manipulate or alter it. Simply accept your surroundings as they present themselves.

☆ It is a still, warm night. The moon is full and bright in a star-encrusted sky. You notice a building in the distance. You approach it knowing that what it contains is significant for you at this moment in your life. It appears to be a museum or library of some sort. There is a light in one of the windows, but no-one seems to be inside. You try the front door and find it unlocked. You enter and find yourself in a spacious hall facing a large notice which reads 'Today's Exhibition: The Life of …'. In the space is your own name.

☆ You walk through into the first gallery which is labelled 'Part One'. Here are preserved the main events in your life so far, not for judging, but rather for detached observation so that all those who visit here can learn about how the spirit fares in the physical world. The most significant episodes, positive and negative as we would see them, are set aside as tableaux in glass cabinets or sculpted in stone and arranged on plinths in alcoves with the relevant dates.

☆ You survey the achievements of your life so far with justifiable pride and note the less positive aspects as moments to learn from. Do not be afraid to review these experiences as they cannot harm you now. You are a detached observer of your own life.

☆ As you come to the closed doors marked with an exit sign at the end of this first gallery, pause and reflect on what you have seen, on the pattern of your life which is now becoming apparent to you as it has not done so before. Pay particular attention to the crucial decisions or crises in your life and consider whether you might have been guided to making a particular decision which determined your future, or if you might have received unexpected help at a critical moment. Can you honestly say that the help or guidance you received then was pure coincidence, or can you imagine that your guardian angel intervened to light your path through life?

☆ Just as you are about to leave you notice an open book set upon a lectern to one side. You glance across to it and see what is written there. It might be a comment on your past actions or advice for the future.

☆ You open the door and pass through into a small lobby entrance or hallway. Across the way is another set of doors. Above these is a sign bearing the inscription 'Part Two'. You have created the exhibitions on display in the first gallery. What would you like to find inside if you were allowed to continue into the second?

☆ An intense white light is streaming from under the door. Your guardian angel is waiting within to show you the future. Have no fear; fear, frustration and regrets are all behind you, dead exhibits with no power to influence the present. Trust your guardian angel to show you your true potential with which you will create your future.

☆ Enter the second room. What do you see there? Do not worry if you do not see the angel. You should, however, sense its presence, even hear its voice inside your mind. What do you learn from this view of the future? What can you do now to bring it into being?

☆ When you are ready, thank your guardian angel for showing you this vision and return to waking consciousness.

☆ Become aware of your surroundings once again, sense your body sitting in the chair and focus on your breathing. Count down slowly from ten to one and open your eyes.

# 4

# Angels and Demons

## An Encounter with the Dark Side

Angels not only have to deal with the troubles we humans get ourselves into, but if the following encounter is to be believed, they must also combat the efforts of the sinister forces which seek to undermine their work.

The encounter was described by a friend of mine (I shall call her Jane for the purpose of this account) whose honesty and sincerity I have no reason to question. Jane was actively engaged in 'rescue work', that is helping restless spirits of the recently deceased to enter the light of the heavenly realms. On the day on which this particular incident occurred she and a close friend had gone to a remote part of the English countryside, an area of natural beauty which attracts walkers, picnicking families and tourists, but few other visitors.

At one particular spot they sensed a disturbing presence who they were able to communicate with and who it appeared was the unquiet spirit of a young woman knocked down and killed at that spot some months before. The suddenness of her death had been such a shock to her psyche that she had not been able to accept that she was no longer alive, and to make matters worse she was troubled by personal matters which remained unresolved. The combination was enough to confine her to the fatal spot.

Jane and her friend were able to put her at rest and after doing so they went to a nearby roadside café for coffee and to get their strength back. The café was deserted, but while they were queuing for food they were overcome by a sense of something cold and ominous approaching. A few moments later two men came in and stood by the entrance staring intently at the women with emotionless features and lifeless eyes.

Jane and her friend went to a table at the far end of the café and sat down, aware that the men were still standing by the entrance and staring intently at them as if to intimidate them. My friend is not of a nervous nature – her psychic and spiritual experiences have shown her that the more she knows, the less she has to fear – but she found the presence of these men disturbing, and it was not because she felt physically threatened. She called inwardly for angelic protection, surrounding herself and her friend in a cocoon of light, and from that moment she sensed that the men were on the defensive. They turned their gaze to the floor and moved aside, allowing the two women to walk smartly past them and out of the café.

It was then, as they paused for breath by the roadside, that Jane sensed a powerful and malevolent presence rushing up behind them. Before she could turn to face it both she and her friend felt a physical force push them out into the road and into the path of a speeding car which had hurtled round the bend to their right. In the split second before it could hit them they were hurtled backwards to safety by another force pushing from the front. As they steadied themselves they watched the car roar down the road and out of sight. In Jane's opinion the driver had been intent on killing them, called upon presumably by his two associates in the café, but her angelic protection proved the stronger and they were saved.

## The Esoteric Tradition

Encounters with the dark forces, such as the one described, raise the eternal question concerning the existence of 'good' and 'evil'. If angels can intervene in our lives, could there also be a consciously malevolent power at work in the world with whom they have had to battle since the creation? Or is evil simply a manifestation of our own inhumanity and the shadow side of the psyche?

While the modern mind is loathe to accept the ancient myths and biblical fables at face value, primarily because in these tales the function of celestial messengers seems to be limited to endorsing the sanctity of the saints and prophets, the darkest episodes of human history suggest that evil does exist in some form. But if the religious texts are suspect, the ancient myths are mere fantasy and the words of the great philosophers are pure conjecture, where can we find reliable descriptions of the invisible realms and their inhabitants?

The answers, I suggest, are to be found encoded in the teachings of the esoteric tradition; that living archive of occult wisdom developed over millennia by the mystics and the secret fraternities of East and West, who shared a common view of this greater reality evolved through personal experience, revelation and insight.

Central to all of these secret schools is one universal truth which is most simply expressed in the ancient Hermetic axiom: 'as above, so below'. This sums up a view of existence in which our physical world is a reflection of the upper worlds, albeit in a denser form. It also implies that these invisible realms are inhabited by a hierarchy of discarnate life forms corresponding to the infinite variety of life on earth. This view of creation is at least logical and in accord with the laws of nature, even if it is not possible for each of us to verify every detail to our satisfaction. It should at least serve as a working hypothesis because the full picture must be denied to us for as long as we are confined to the physical body.

If we are to work with angels we first have to know what else, if anything, is 'out there', and how it might attempt to interfere, distract or disturb our efforts. We must face our own fears, our inner demons, before we can launch ourselves into uncharted territory with the best of intentions but perhaps little idea about what we might encounter when we get there.

## Elementals

It is my understanding, sustained by insight and experience, that elementals, the natural inhabitants of the lower worlds, are not malevolent but merely of a lower nature. They can be compared to what were once known as the 'dumb beasts' of the animal kingdom, and are believed to take as many forms as there are species of animals on earth. For example, those who are on a level of development comparable to the primates could be seen as acting like mischievous monkeys or wilful young children, ruled by their impulses and instincts. None of these evolving forms are harmful to humans, but they should be ignored if encountered during an out-of-body experience, or if their presence is sensed during any form of psychic work. They may not bite, but to the unprepared their appearance can be extremely disturbing, as anyone who has suffered hallucinations through alcohol or drug abuse could testify. It is my own personal belief that hallucinations are temporary glimpses into these lower worlds, precipitated by the lowering of the mind's fail-safe sensory mechanism.

In the normal course of events we are unaware of these lower levels and their inhabitants; they are confined to their habitat as we are to ours. It is only when we drift out of our bodies into the astral dimension during sleep, or if we actively expand our awareness into other dimensions through meditation, that we *might* encounter them, although it is only a very remote possibility for the natural inclination of the human spirit is ascent back to the Divine.

If you are at all anxious about working with angels, remember that at all times we have continual, unconditional protection both from our guardian angels and by virtue of our innate Divinity, which no creature can corrupt or violate.

## Thought Forms

More potentially dangerous are the thought forms that people have brought into being on the astral plane, consciously or unconsciously, through the intensity of their thoughts and emotions. In the normal course of events our thoughts form fleeting impressions on the astral plane from the discharge of mental energy. They immediately disperse into the ether like a cloud of cigarette smoke. However, if they are charged with intense emotion over a prolonged period, such as when we have recurring thoughts about someone whom we either love or extremely dislike, we can charge that thought form with so much energy that it takes on a life of its own, though it remains without consciousness. In extreme cases it can become a parasite, sucking the energy from those who gave it life.

I know of one group of young men who became so obsessed with a popular fantasy role-playing game that they unconsciously created a thought form from the energy they were expending regularly and intensely on the game. When one of my psychic friends visited them one evening she was horrified to 'see' this thing, which looked like a pulsating black cloud, hovering over the group and feeding on their emotional and mental energy. When she suggested to one of the group that such an obsession might be unhealthy (not daring to tell him what she had seen), he reacted like an addict deprived of his fix. He freely admitted to being obsessed by his fantasy, but said that they all got a buzz from it which drew them back again and again. Unknown to them this thrill was a stimulus from the entity to ensure that it would continue to be fed.

Role-playing games are not dangerous in themselves (another group I know played the game for years in a spirit of fun and had no ill effects whatsoever), but anything which serves as a focus for intense negative emotion has the potential to be harmful, whether it is graphic horror fiction, extreme nationalism, a personality cult, religious fundamentalism or even the nightly TV crime reports which exploit our fears and fascination with the dark side of our psyche.

In contrast, places of worship are often centres of positive thought forms charged by prayer and spiritual aspirations. You can sense this energy field in many churches, mosques, synagogues and temples even if you do not subscribe to the particular belief. The sense of serenity and the sacred can suffuse the atmosphere of such places as densely as a cloud of incense, hence angels are often seen in such places as they are the embodiment of this energy, which takes form according to the unconscious will and expectations of the witness.

*We are what we think.*
*All that we are arises with our thoughts.*
*With our thoughts we make the world.*
*Speak and act with an impure mind*
*And trouble will follow you*
*As the wheel follows the ox that draws the cart.*
The Dhammapada (the moral teachings of the Buddha)

## Good and Evil

Our belief in the existence of angels and demons is confused by our need to believe in good and evil. If we can accept instead that good and evil are human concepts developed to bring order to society and give meaning to our existence, then angels and demons can be accepted as being simply higher and lower forms in nature's hierarchy, rather than as soldiers in some mythical battle for the souls of helpless human beings. The word demon is an unfortunate one as it has religious connotations. It is actually a corruption of the Greek word *daimon* which translates simply as 'spirit' or 'deity'.

In many pagan traditions, and in Eastern philosophies such as Taoism and Buddhism, evil is viewed as the contrary impulse, the force of contraction necessary to contain the inexorable momentum of an eternally unfolding universe. In the Western esoteric tradition, which is based on the Jewish mystical teaching known as Kabbalah, this concept is expanded to take in the idea that evil is the impulse for destruction, disintegration, decay and death which are the natural processes of life. It is only when human beings consciously and wilfully destroy what God has given life that true evil is born. If we consciously choose to act contrary to the will of God, we are abusing the gift of free will which distinguishes us from all other forms of life, including the angels.

I personally cannot believe in the existence of evil as a conscious entity in a universe which is the expression of a loving God. As I stated in my book, *Kabbalah* 'that which is perfect cannot create something which is imperfect'. What we perceive as evil are the evil acts of our fellow human beings, which occur because they are not conscious of their Divine nature and are temporarily insensitive to its influence. Evil is the lack of conscience caused by separation from the source.

The existence of angels does not automatically signify the existence of demons. If angels are the highest form of discarnate beings, surely they are complemented by the lower, undeveloped forms I have described, and not necessarily by conscious beings of equal strength but contrary nature. The number of angelic encounters which have been reported are overwhelming, they cross all boundaries of religion, race, culture and belief and are remarkably consistent in content. In contrast, no-one of sound mind has claimed to have seen a devil or demon since the Middle Ages. They have not even been seen at the sites of natural disasters, accidents or human atrocities. As for evil spirits, I see these as the spirits of disturbed human beings or products of the human mind.

It would seem that the devils of old are merely figments of our fevered imaginations and projections of our guilt and fears. The real demons, I suggest, are of our own making. If that is so, we have nothing to fear but our own shadows.

## Angels of Protection

Following on from the discussion of thought forms, the following exercises describe how you can create an angelic thought form of your own to protect your home from intruders. I can personally vouch for the effectiveness of the first visualisation, having used it to deter burglars and vandals when I was living in a particularly rough neighbourhood. My neighbours' houses were fitted with burglar alarms but were continually being broken into, the wheels of their cars were periodically stolen and their walls and fences vandalised. Thanks to the angelic protection my house remained secure during the entire time that I lived there, while I enjoyed the peace of mind that goes with being in the company of the angels. Moreover, I saved the considerable expense of having to install a burglar and car alarm and the nuisance caused by having them go off for no reason in the middle of the night.

## EXERCISE: ANGELIC PROTECTION

☆ Begin as usual by focusing on your breathing. Work through the tuning in meditation described in Chapter 1, and when you feel sufficiently relaxed focus your attention on the soles of your feet. In your mind's eye visualise the floor dissolving and the energy from Mother Earth being absorbed through the soles of your feet. You should begin to feel a tingling sensation or heat after a few moments. Work your way up through the body in small stages – the lower legs, thighs, solar plexus and so on – taking about one minute to focus on each point. Feel the energy rising very gradually through your body as if you are soaking it up. Visualise a milky white or golden light enveloping you so that by the time you reach the crown of your head you are illuminated and energised from top to toe.

☆ Then draw the celestial energy in through the crown of your head with each inhalation and visualise the two streams of energy mixing harmoniously within the very centre of your being. Now begin to draw that energy together at the third eye centre between your brows, at the heart centre in the middle of your chest and at the solar plexus centre beneath your navel. When you can feel the heat concentrated in those three centres or a tingling sensation at each centre, begin to project the energy as swirls of smoke or, if you prefer, as beams of light, a few feet away from you, about two arms' length.

The energy from the brow centre will give the figure form and imprint it with your will and purpose, the energy from the heart centre will in a sense 'ensoul' it with an aspect of your personality, while the energy from the solar plexus will effectively animate it with physical energy.

Visualise the energy taking the form of a winged angel with a mighty sword who will reach from floor to ceiling. Alternatively, those of you old enough to remember a British TV rock show called the *Old Grey Whistle Test* might like to use the image that opened the programme – a featureless figure of white light arising from the flames of a fire and stretching out its arms like a dancer preparing to take flight. This is a very simple but effective image to conjure up and one which is almost impossible to invest with anything other than positive vibrations.

☆ When you have the angelic image fixed in your mind, send it about its task with a set of clear instructions to protect your property from those who would wish you ill and for a fixed time limit (for example, 'until daylight', 'until I return home this evening' or 'until I return from my holiday on such and such a date'). This latter point is very important as you do not wish to risk creating a thought form which could take on a life and personality of its own. This phenomenon has been known to happen to people with even the most honourable of intentions, such as the Buddhist llama Alexandra David-Neel.

☆ Remember also to instruct the angel not to harm anybody, even those of evil intent, and that it exists at all times under the laws and will of God. When the allotted time is up you should enter a meditative state and visualise drawing your angel back into the room and reabsorbing the energy. When you are ready, return to waking consciousness.

This ability to focus your consciousness in another area of your body takes time and practice, because we are used to believing that consciousness resides in the physical brain. It does not. We are consciousness personified and need to train our minds to refocus on the other energy centres. This will become easier with practise and the visualisation as a whole can then be completed in a few minutes so that you can set your angelic protection as easily as you would set the burglar alarm.

## Psychic Force Fields

Partners, friends, family and people with no intent to cause you or your property injury will be able to pass the angelic guards without a problem, as they will be in harmony with, or at least neutral to, the energy pattern you have created, although do not be surprised if they comment on having noticed an improvement in the atmosphere.

If you feel unsettled or insecure for any reason, however, try the following additional remedy:

☆ Empty a packet of coarse salt on to a plate or tray and charge it with positive energy by holding your hands over it and working through the tuning in meditation.

☆ Feel the energy flowing through your body and out of your fingertips into the salt. In your mind's eye see it glowing with positive life force as you invoke the help of the angels using your own words.

☆ Then sprinkle a trail of the charged coarse salt around the boundaries of your property while appealing for the angels to protect you and your home in words of your own choosing.

It is important while performing this ritual that you think of the salt being formed into a barrier of positive energy, a type of invisible force field, and not in terms of an electric barrier that will cause harm, even to unwanted intruders. Esoteric tradition informs us that it would be better to allow a determined burglar to get away with a few possessions than to will any harm upon someone, as that would incur a karmic debt to be repaid at a future date or even in a future lifetime.

If someone is ever able to force their way through your invisible barrier, which is extremely unlikely, it could be because you let your guard down, so to speak, by neglecting to give the visualisation the full focus of your attention or the strength of your convictions. This is not a cop-out on my behalf; energy fields are created on the astral level and a physical body can bludgeon its way through if it is sufficiently determined or insensitive to the discouraging charge in the atmosphere. But as my own experience shows, the casual opportunist thief or mindless vandal should feel distinctly uncomfortable when they approach a protected sacred space, and may even sense a presence that is sufficiently strong to put them off.

If you are unfortunate enough to have your home broken into you can rid yourself of the disturbance in the atmosphere with the salt in the same way that you laid your invisible barrier. Above all, resist the temptation to indulge in ill-feeling towards the intruder as this will ultimately rebound on you. Take comfort in the fact that your intruder will have taken upon themselves a karmic burden that they will one day be called to repay, while you will receive comfort. And if you learn from the experience to channel your anger in a safe manner, know that in time you will receive much more than could ever have been taken from you.

## Self-Protection

Even if you are physically strong and feel confident that you can take care of yourself, it is still good policy to avail yourself of angelic protection on a daily basis. It is not a case of expecting disaster or of giving in to your anxieties, but a simple matter of putting yourself on the side of the angels so that you are not caught offguard by events and start the day centred, secure in yourself and confident that all will be well.

Once you are familiar with the following exercise it can be done in a few moments, but always give it your full attention. Even when it becomes part of your routine do not allow it to become a mere habit, but cultivate the state of heightened awareness which the Buddhists call 'mindfulness'. If you are appealing for Divine protection or guidance such exercises must always be performed as a sacred act.

## EXERCISE: THE ANGEL'S CLOAK AND CONSORTS

This exercise is best performed standing up.

☆ Begin the visualisation as usual by focusing on your breathing, then when you are suitably relaxed and centred visualise a point of white light in the centre of your forehead. Feel it growing in size and in intensity until it spreads across your forehead, eventually extending several inches beyond your shoulders.

Now imagine that you reach up and grip this halo of light with invisible hands (your physical body remains still during this 'astral exercise'), then pull it down slowly around you until it rests on the floor leaving a blur of light all around you. You are now standing within a protective cylinder of light and energy. Your own energy and aura are encased within this invisible halo preventing them from being drained by others, while their negative thoughts and energy are unable to penetrate your protection and disturb you. Be clear that this is not a means for you to withdraw from the world, however, but rather to remain 'in the world but not of it' to borrow another Buddhist saying.

☆ If you wish you can imagine the light taking the form of a full-length hooded cloak with boots and gloves of light. Wrap the light around yourself to seal your aura and then, if you feel the need of extra protection for a particular journey or have some reason for anxiety, appeal to the archangels to guard and guide you using the following invocation or one of your own choosing:

*'Heavenly Father, as a spark of thy eternal flame, incarnate in thy service, I ask for the guidance and protection of thy Divine messengers.*

*May Raphael go before me, Gabriel behind me, Michael by my right hand and Uriel by my left hand, whilst above me shines the six-rayed star, sign of the Living Presence of God, to illumine my true path to my true place in peace.'*

☆ Return to waking consciousness confident in the belief that you have invoked the highest guidance and protection possible. Quite apart from protecting you against any physical danger or emotional disturbances which you may have encountered, this invocation will make you mindful of the Divine presence in your life so that you do not fritter the day away as you might otherwise have done.

# 5

# Making Contact

*Ask, and it shall be given you; seek and ye shall find; knock and it shall be opened unto you.*

Matthew (7:7)

One of the most curious aspects of human nature is our tendency (perhaps habit would be a more accurate term) to dwell on negative thoughts when there is every reason to expect a positive future and a degree of fulfilment in our lives. For most of us our fears of failure, of suffering serious illness and sudden catastrophe are in complete contrast to our present condition. Such fatalistic and ultimately self-defeating impulses are the result of a lifetime of subtle conditioning, of an insidious poisoning of the psyche which can undermine our happiness and enjoyment of life, but which we can rid ourselves of with the assistance of the angels and in so doing turn our 'luck' and our lives around.

This kind of conditioning, to which we have all been exposed to a certain degree, has in effect 'programmed' us to expect a life as melodramatic and contrived as a soap opera. It also denies our innate Divinity and the degree of free will which we all possess. If these fears are indulged they may well come to fruition, if only to demonstrate the power of the human mind to create what it unconsciously seeks to confront.

## Asking for Angelic Assistance

We like to imagine that angels are alert to our every need and forever 'on call', because this image serves our yearning for a sense of purpose in life and a longing for unconditional love. The love of God and His administering angels may indeed be unconditional, but this does not necessarily infer that either likes to be taken for granted. From personal experiences and those of other people who claim to have been helped at critical moments in their life by the angelics, it would appear that they like to be asked. It's almost as if by asking we are acknowledging their existence and showing faith in their ability and willingness to help. Even the most devoted, selfless and loving parent needs to have their love returned now and then, and as the major religions are so fond of talking of humanity in terms of being children of God, I suggest that a Heavenly Father and His administering angels will respond in much the same way.

The following exercises describe how to ask the angels for help with specific problems in a way which guarantees a response.

### EXERCISE: IMPROVING RELATIONSHIPS

If you are involved in a difficult relationship with someone to whom you are emotionally attached, such as a partner, family member or close friend, you can help to dispel any disharmony between you by practis- ing the following simple exercise on a regular basis.

After only a short time you should see the relationship from a new, less emotional perspective, and the other person will be affected too, although on a subtle, psychic level which they will not be consciously aware of. It is imperative, however, that you do not divulge what you have done to improve your relationship to any one, particularly not to the person concerned, as there is a real danger that they might consider themselves to have been manipulated in some way.

☆ Make yourself comfortable in a chair and settle into a meditative state by focusing on your breathing and scanning your body from crown to toes for tension. Then take a deep breath and sigh, expelling all the tension with the out-breath.

☆ When you feel suitably relaxed ask for your guardian angel to draw near and assist you for the highest good of all concerned. It is important to include this phrase because the success of any healing process depends on harmonising with the greater good and the will of the universal creative force, rather than imposing your will or manifesting the desires of your ego. Visualise your guardian angel appearing behind you and wrapping you in its wings of multi-coloured auric light.

☆ Now see the other person approaching from a distance, gently guided by their guardian angel who stands behind them. When they finally stand before you sense your heart centre soften and open with unconditional love for this other person and ask your angel to communicate your wish to heal any ill-feeling between the two of you. Ask too for forgiveness for any hurt which you may have inadvertently caused and ask for any karmic debt that exists between you to be cleared for the highest good of all concerned.

☆ Then see the wings of both angels unfold and touch to form a circle of light enclosing you and the other person. Now visualise yourself breathing that person in with every in-breath. Embrace and absorb that person into the essence of your own being and say the following affirmation to yourself: 'X and I are having a good, positive relationship. Energy flows freely between us.' When you exhale, visualise yourself releasing them back into the embrace of their guardian angel.

☆ Repeat the exercise as many times as you feel necessary, then thank both angels for bringing you together and assisting in the healing process. Sense them returning from whence they came, focus on your breathing, and when you are ready return to waking consciousness.

(To free yourself of a non-productive relationship see 'The Angel of the Moon' exercise on page 96.)

## The Papal Angel

There is an intriguing story concerning one of the Catholic popes who was known for his unusual method of dissolving a potential crisis. It is a simple method which you may find useful in dissolving your own problems.

Whenever he was due to meet someone who he expected might be difficult to deal with, the pope would appeal to his guardian angel to intercede on his behalf. He would ask his own guardian angel to speak with the other person's guardian angel and resolve whatever difficulties might arise between them before the meeting took place. Although the pope's name is not known it is said that his papacy was particularly noted for its great diplomatic achievements.

You might care to try his method the next time you anticipate a confrontation. You may find that even if the other party doesn't appear to have had a change of heart, or be keen to compromise, the fact that you consulted your own guardian angel will have given you a fresh perspective on the problem, or simply made you less defensive or intense.

The following exercise is designed to ask the angels to help with the release of negative energies and suppressed emotions such as the unburdening of guilt or regrets, but it can also be adapted to ask for guidance or insight on specific problems.

## EXERCISE: THE ANGEL OF FORGIVENESS

Begin as usual with the basic relaxation, grounding and clearing exercise from Chapter 2.

☆ When you feel sufficiently relaxed visualise yourself standing on a mountain top where the air is clear, fresh and invigorating. Far below, the clouds obscure the earth from view. On a ledge just below you mountain goats graze on exotic-coloured flowers which grow through the cracks in the stone. The tinkling of the bells around the necks of the goats is the only sound you can hear in the stillness.

☆ You turn away from the edge and walk across the plateau to where a small wooden bridge straddles a sparkling stream. You begin to cross, pausing half-way to enjoy the sound of the running water which lulls you into an even deeper state of relaxation. Finally you step on to the other side where stands a small temple to which you feel irresistibly drawn. You climb ten steps and enter the temple where the feeling of serenity and well-being is almost overwhelming. The scent of incense and flowers is intoxicating. Everywhere candles are burning with not a breath of wind to unsteady their flame. All is stillness and serenity.

☆ To each side sit a line of people just like you in quiet contemplation. They bow their heads with respect in acknowledgement of your presence as you enter and walk towards the altar which lies at the far end of the temple. Before the altar are baskets of fruit and flowers and pictures of the angels who have served and guided all those who have come to the temple this day. Perhaps you respond to one of these celestial beings?

☆ You bow before an awesome statue of an archangel which rises behind the altar, but this is not idol worship, you are acknowledging the Divine potential in yourself which it symbolises. On the floor in front of you is a cushion with sheaves of paper and a pen. Kneel down and open your heart centre in this sacred space, allowing whatever troubles you to rise up and find expression in words or perhaps even in a symbol of some sort. Feel it being plucked like a stone from the emotional centre of your being as you write down your thoughts, your plea for forgiveness, or your question. Now, what do you replace the empty space with? What do you take from this place of peace and forgiveness?

☆ See yourself folding the paper into a taper and placing it in the flame of a candle which lies by the feet of the angel statue. Watch the paper blacken and see the smoke rise into the shaft of light which breaks through the window above the angel's head. Drop the ash into a bowl of water and know that you are relieved of guilt or of whatever has been needlessly troubling you. Accept that any mistakes you made were an essential part of your learning in life and forgive yourself. Know too that in asking you are forgiven and relieved of this burden now and for ever. If you asked a question know with certainty that the answer will come, perhaps during your dreams this night.

☆ Now gradually become aware of your surroundings once again, sense your body sitting in the chair and focus on your breathing. Count down slowly from ten to one and when you are ready, open your eyes.

## Angelic Awareness

The following exercise is designed to encourage you to stop and think before acting rashly in a difficult situation. We all tend to react instinctively to a perceived threat, particularly if it is to our ego and if we feel that we have been treated unfairly. Such reactions are natural, they are part of our defensive survival mechanism, but emotionally, mentally and psychically it is we who suffer by winding ourselves up into a knot of negative emotion instead of letting go. Acting in the heat of the moment can often make a difficult situation even worse; frequently we react by saying something that we later regret and it is usually we who suffer the consequences rather than the person we thought was in the wrong. Here is an instant method of defusing a potentially volatile situation.

## EXERCISE: THE ANGELIC BODYGUARD

☆ Take a deep breath, pushing out the diaphragm, and visualise a powerful light beaming down upon you as if a spotlight had been switched on, flooding you with light. The breath will still and centre you so that you are no longer caught offguard but have a second or two to think. The light will remind you that you are both Divine beings in essence and share the same Father/Mother creator, although your antagonist is evidently not conscious of it at that moment, and being Divine you have a responsibility not to create friction, fear or hurt.

☆ Then invoke the angel with whom you feel an affinity using the following words: 'Archangel Michael, protector and guide, let your light shine through me and your presence go before me.' Or you can ask for your own guardian angel by altering the invocation to: 'In the name of the Most High let the light of my guardian angel shine through me and its presence go before me.'

Having done this you will not be able to react in an equally hostile fashion to your antagonist because you will have invoked the highest aspect of your personality and restrained the lowest, the ego. It may take some practice for this procedure to become second nature, but it will be worth it for it is of little value being saintly and compassionate when the situation suits us if we give in to our baser instincts when we are out in the real world.

However, if the antagonist is a serious threat rather than just a nuisance, visualise drawing the cloak of light about you and invoke the four archangels as described in the exercise 'The Angel's Cloak and Consorts' in Chapter 4. See them surrounding you and call on Divine protection to come to your aid. Your distress call will not be ignored.

## *Clearing Resentment*

Equally challenging and rather more serious for your own health and peace of mind is a situation in which you feel that you have been criticised unfairly or taken for granted and are left burning on a slow fuse without having had the opportunity to tell your side of the story. Perhaps someone in authority, such as a boss, colleague or teacher, has been undermining your efforts and you feel unable to respond, or maybe a stranger said something which you can't seem to shake out of your mind even though you know there is no point worrying about it. You can also use this method to clear any long-standing resentment safely and effectively without injuring the person who you believe was responsible for hurting you.

If you feel there is a genuine cause for grievance and have a serious case to put then common sense will dictate what action you take, but in most cases it is our pride that has been hurt and our egos that have been bruised. Yet even trivial matters can give rise to resentment that can eat away at our insides and cause ill-health, so it must be cleared and our sense of balance and peace of mind restored.

This can be achieved by carrying out the following exercise.

### EXERCISE: THE ANGELIC COUNSELLOR

☆ Find a place where you will not be disturbed and if necessary take the phone off the hook. Take with you a pen, paper and envelope, a candle, matches and a tin box (such as a biscuit tin) half-filled with water.

☆ Perform the tuning in exercise described in Chapter 1 to balance, ground and centre yourself, then light the candle and invoke your guardian angel with these or similar words: *'In the name of the Most High I ask for the blessing of the loving presence of my Holy Guardian Angel at this hour of need. I put into its hands this matter and ask that it be resolved for the highest good of all concerned.'*

☆ Now place the writing paper in front of you and take up the pen. Close your eyes for a few moments and visualise your guardian angel standing behind you. See it in as much detail as possible and feel its hands upon your shoulders offering you its understanding, guidance and courage. Ask it quietly for guidance in this matter and in the certain knowledge that you will receive it. When you are ready write your letter to the person who has upset you, telling them of your feelings and explaining the situation as you see it. It is as important to tell them how you feel as it is to state your grievance, as the primary purpose of this exercise is to clear your emotional bond to this person, not to restore your sense of justice. Write carefully and with the intent of communicating with this person wherever they are in the world. You can even do this exercise if the other person has passed into the spirit world. Try to visualise them as you do this to strengthen the psychic bond.

☆ As you write be aware that your angel is looking over your shoulder. This should help you to express yourself succinctly and avoid creating further animosity, while giving you a sense that you have had a sympathetic hearing. In the sacred presence of the angel you should hopefully become aware that the situation was perhaps not as one-sided as you had imagined, that it may have stemmed from a misunderstanding or that you now feel able to forgive and forget.

☆ When you have finished, fold and address the envelope (putting a description of the person if you do not know their name), and seal it as if you were going to post it. Then, while asking your guardian angel to take this message and your feelings with it into the light, burn the envelope in the candle flame and drop it into the water-filled tin. Thank your angel and extinguish the candle. Have confidence that your negative emotional energy has been dispersed safely into the ether and the matter has been given over to the angels.

> *Everything we call a trial, a sorrow, or a duty;*
> *Believe me, that Angel's hand is there.*
> Fra Giovanni

# 6

# The Angels of the Elements

Contacting the Angels of Fire, Air, Water and Earth increases our awareness of the four elements traditionally considered to be the primary constituents of the cosmos. In human terms these correspond to the will (fire), intellect (air), emotions (water) and the physical body (earth). In esoteric teachings water and earth are viewed as symbolic of the passive, feminine principle, while fire and air represent the active, masculine principle.

You can also invoke the Archangel Michael who is the Lord of the Sun and symbol of healing, regeneration and renewal. He is also known as the Prince of Heaven and can be called upon to assist you in achieving your ambitions and aspirations. His companion is Gabriel, Lord of the Moon, who you can appeal to to help you develop your intuition and imagination.

## The Angel of Earth

Contacting the Angel of Earth reminds us of the importance of grounding ourselves, of keeping our feet firmly in the physical. Visualisations such as the one described below enforce this idea upon the unconscious mind, which communicates solely in symbols. Too often people who practice meditation become 'bliss junkies' and forget their purpose and responsibilities in life. Contacting the Angel of Earth on a regular basis will remind you that meditation is not an escape from reality but a method of channelling angelic power and guidance to enrich your life and focus your attention in the 'real world'.

The Angel of Earth can also be contacted when you feel the need to draw upon the practical aspect of your nature, increase your concentration or stimulate the determination to see something through. If you are given to daydreams, frustrated in your ambitions or feel that you are undermined by irrational impulses, compulsions and bad habits, calling upon this angel should restore balance and a sense of perspective as it is a symbol of stability. If, however, you fear that you are too preoccupied with earthly or material matters and are becoming bogged down with detail or chained to commitments, concentrate on contacting the angels of the other three elements. Ask for their assistance and imagine yourself being pulled out of a hole that you have dug for yourself. Crude symbols such as this are often the most effective way of asking the unconscious to yank the conscious mind out of a rut and to convey the urgency of the situation to the angels through the mirror of the imagination.

## EXERCISE: THE ANGEL OF EARTH

Make yourself comfortable and begin by focusing on your breathing.

☆ When you feel suitably relaxed visualise yourself standing in a forest clearing on a pleasantly warm morning with the sun streaming through the tall trees.

☆ You are going to build a sanctuary for yourself to which you can return whenever you feel the need to take a rest from the pressures of modern life. When you have done this in detail as you would in physical reality, then you can invoke the Angel of Earth to sanctify it and abide in this place of peace so that whenever you return to this sacred place in the inner mind the angelic energy will be there for you to draw upon and channel into your waking existence. Begin by visualising all the tools and materials that you will need. Call each to mind and see them materialise before you. When you have all you need, begin to build your sanctuary. Take your time and see it through all the stages.

☆ When you have built your sanctuary furnish it to your liking and create an altar at which you will honour the Angel of Earth whose presence pervades this sacred place. If you believe that you lack the self-discipline and determination needed to see things through in the waking world, then drawing upon the angel's guidance and strength will help focus your attention in the future.

☆ Now look up at the sunlight streaming through the window on to your altar and visualise the Angel of Earth manifesting from the heart of this soft, golden light as you say these words or others of your own choosing:

'Angel of Earth, I ask for the blessing of your loving presence here in this place at this time for the purpose of healing and illumination. Come as you will in the form of your choosing,

> *but always with the blessing and at the behest of the*
> *Almighty, blessed be He.'*

Sense its presence which is the manifestation of unconditional love, and as you stand in the shadow of its protective wings ask for the Divine qualities which it embodies to be awakened and strengthened in yourself.

☆ When you have communicated all that you wish to say, thank the angel for its blessing and for heeding your summons at your time of need. Then visualise it returning to the light, and when you are ready become aware once again of your surroundings and open your eyes.

## The Angel of Air

The Angel of Air can be seen as both the personification of the intellect and of the animating spirit which finds expression in the breath – that which Hindus call prana, or the life force. If you find your vitality drained and you are under stress, you can appeal to the Angel of Air to dispel the cloud of negativity surrounding you and to breathe the revitalising force into every cell of your being. This will reanimate the chakras (the subtle energy centres in the etheric body), restore the flow of prana and help to avert disease.

It is equally important to maintain a balance between thought and emotion so that your mind remains clear and is not clouded by fear and anxiety. If you are feeling low or even depressed, put everything back into perspective using the visualisation below, in which the angel will carry you up to the clouds from where you can watch the teeming multitudes struggling with problems that will have no meaning to them in a month from now.

If you are plagued by dreams or fears of your house being buffeted by strong winds it could be a sign that you need to appeal to the Angel of Air to restore a sense of security and help you to cool down the flames of irrational and intense emotions. Many cultures preserve myths of gods who sent their messages on the winds. This universal archetypal image can be used by the unconscious to convey an important message to the waking mind, so don't dismiss the image of an angelic messenger or its message if it appears in your meditation or dreams.

## EXERCISE: THE ANGEL OF AIR

☆ Begin the visualisation by focusing on your breathing as usual, then take a deep breath, sigh, and expel all the tension throughout your body. Return to regular breathing, and as you do so imagine that you are sitting in the shade of the ruins of an ancient temple which is half-buried in sand in the midst of a vast, silent desert.

☆ Contemplate the passing of time and the impermanence of all material things which has consigned this once great civilisation to the dust. Over the centuries the bitterly cold desert nights have cracked the smooth surface of the pillars and sandstorms have scoured the symbols from the walls and defaced the features of the statues. This is the fate of all attempts by human beings to impose their will on the elements.

☆ The structure has been reduced to an empty shell, but it is pervaded by a powerful presence which you can now sense is drawing near as it desires to communicate some of the secrets that were once taught here. You invoke this being by asking it to share some of its secrets for your guidance and highest good:

*'Angel of Air, I ask for the blessing of your loving presence here in this place at this time for the purpose of healing and illumination. Come as you will in the form of your choosing but always with the blessing and at the behest of the Almighty, blessed be He.'*

☆ Shield your eyes from the intense bright light that now envelops you and willingly surrender to its warm embrace. You can sense the span of its mighty wings enfolding you as you are absorbed into the light.

☆ In the next moment, sense yourself rising, carried into the air by the angel high above the desert and in a cloudless sky. The breeze caresses your face as you rise higher and higher, and when you look down you can see the desert caravans of the nomadic tribes snaking across the sands to the cities by the sea.

☆ In the angel's embrace you glide between the minarets to gaze down upon the citizens of the world doing business in the bazaars, worshipping in their holy places and discussing politics, philosophy and the transitory preoccupations of their lives wherever they meet another person of like mind. It all seems so intensely important to them, but to you, in the presence of this timeless being, the affairs of the world are of little concern. Their harsh words are scattered by the wind, the heat of their emotions are cooled by the breeze.

☆ In the harbour the sails of the merchant ships billow,

filled with the wind that will carry them across the sea to distribute their goods, their provisions and knowledge to the people of distant lands. It is the same wind that scatters the seeds of trees and plants across the continents to ensure that the cycle of life is unbroken. The wind is symbolic of the momentum of change. It serves the creative force, reminding us that without change there can be no growth. All things have their place and purpose in the fabric of existence, but when each has played its part it too will pass away to be scattered like the desert sand.

☆ Now is the moment to ask the angel for guidance or for healing. When you have received it, thank the angel and ask it to set you down on the earth where you will say your farewell. When you are ready, return to waking consciousness by becoming gradually aware of your surroundings and refocusing on your breathing.

## The Angel of Water

The Angel of the Water influences the fluidity of the emotions and can also help us to plumb the depths of the unconscious. If you are cast adrift on the turbulent waters of your own emotions, or feel overwhelmed by waves of apprehension, you can appeal to the Angel of Water to restore calm, serenity and contentment. Fear of the unknown, or of 'taking the plunge' into a new venture or relationship, can be alleviated by appealing to the angel to illuminate what appear to be deep, fathomless waters and reveal what lies beneath the surface. A variation on this visualisation can help dispel fear of being 'out of one's depth' in a situation, of losing control and being swept along by events.

If the angel is pictured by a stream it can indicate that you are being encouraged to 'go with the flow' rather than 'swim against the tide' of events. Fast-flowing water can symbolise energy which is seeking release, either through physical activity, or a form of self-expression which is an effective means of channelling excess emotional energy. If you suspect that there might be an unconscious barrier to self-expression, such as the fear of failure, the Angel of Water can be invoked to resolve the conflict between the conscious mind and the emotional impulse.

If you feel as if you are being dragged down by the weight of responsibilities, debts or the demands of other people, again, this angel can help, but consider the wording of your request very carefully before entering meditation.

The following visualisation can be used for pure relaxation, and for spiritual and emotional refreshment.

## Exercise: The Angel of Water

Make yourself comfortable and begin by focusing on your breathing.

☆ When you feel suitably relaxed visualise yourself sitting under a tree by a lake surrounded by mountains.

☆ It is the moment before dawn and as you watch the sun rise, its rays turn the calm waters flaming red and orange. As the sun climbs in the sky you feel drawn to walk to the water's edge. Imagine yourself stretching and standing up, leaving behind all your stress and cares. Feel the damp grass under your feet and between your toes. Smell the fresh mountain air and feel the breeze brushing through your hair and over your body. Hear the sound of the birds circling in the sky above you and the distant call of wild animals in the forest behind you.

☆ Walk down to the lake and along the bank, stopping occasionally to bend down and look at the stones and the plants growing by the water's edge. Pick up a stone that attracts you and turn it over in your hand. Run your fingers over its contours and feel the texture of its surface. The water looks cool and inviting. You wade in and find it pleasantly warm. You can still feel the soil between your toes but now you also feel the warmth of the water lapping against your legs.

☆ You wade out a little further where you can see the rocks under the sparkling surface. An exotically coloured fish swims up to you and circles you before swimming away. Perhaps you feel like swimming, but if not you can wade out to where the rocks break the surface and just sit and drink in the stillness and the pleasant warmth of the sun on your head, neck and shoulders.

☆ Whichever you choose to do, this is the time to ask what you will of the angel whose presence pervades this place. If, for example, you are having difficulty making an important decision, visualise yourself looking down into murky water which symbolises clouded judgement and visualise the angel appearing from the depths to purify the water and restore clarity. As you stare into the water and ask for guidance, the answer should appear either in the form of a symbol or from the lips of the angel itself. If not, be assured that it will appear in your dreams or in the form of a hint from a person you know or as a new opportunity which offers a solution.

☆ Invoke the Angel of Water with these words or a similar invocation of your own choosing:

> '*Angel of Water, I ask for the blessing of your loving presence here in this place at this time for the purpose of healing and illumination. Come as you will in the form of your choosing but always with the blessing and at the behest of the Almighty, blessed be He.*'

☆ When you are ready, begin to wade back to the shore. When you reach the bank walk up to the tree and retrieve your everyday clothes, but even as you do so you retain the sense of this revitalising experience and will do for the rest of the day.

☆ Now once again get a sense of your surroundings, of your body sitting in the chair, and when you are ready, open your eyes.

## The Angel of Fire

The Angel of Fire carries the light of knowledge with which it illuminates the darkness of ignorance. It is a purifying force which can be called upon to burn away the crust of conditioning that has desensitised us from greater self-awareness. If it appears as a destructive force in a visualisation it could be that you need to reconsider what is really important to you and what it may be time to discard.

You can appeal to this angel to shed light on long-neglected memories which might appear in meditation as objects found in the shadows of an attic or basement room (both symbols of the unconscious). If you feel emotionally 'cold' at any time you can call on the Angel of Fire to rekindle your passion for life, although if you are subject to a flare up of anger or resentment you might find it necessary to meditate upon the qualities of the other three angels of the elements to dampen or extinguish the flames.

Visualising flames reflected in water as you call upon the respective angels can assist the integration of the active male aspect and the passive feminine aspect which are to be considered complementary and vital for self-realisation.

## EXERCISE: THE ANGEL OF FIRE

Begin as usual by making yourself comfortable, closing your eyes and focusing on your breathing.

☆ When you feel sufficiently relaxed visualise yourself entering a temple in a forest. The temple is deserted, the air still and heavily scented with incense. Take a long look around and take in the details. Perhaps there are sacred statues or designs on the floor and walls which may hold significance for you.

☆ At the far end of the building there is a flight of stone steps leading down into a lower chamber. You descend slowly counting down from ten to one with each step and feeling more relaxed as you descend deeper and deeper into the shadows. When you reach the bottom you are in a very deep state of relaxation and yet more aware and more sensitive to atmosphere than ever before. The sense of peace is all pervading. As your eyes adjust to the half-light you see that the chamber is lit with the light of many candles and that it is bare except for a simple stone altar in the centre. You approach the altar on which burns an eternal flame dedicated to the Angel of Fire. Bow your head and ask for the angel to bless you with its presence and protection using the following invocation or one of your own if you prefer:

*'Angel of Fire, I ask for the blessing of your loving presence here in this place at this time for the purpose of healing and illumination. Come as you will in the form of your choosing but always with the blessing and at the behest of the Almighty, blessed be He.'*

☆ Sense the presence of the angel before you, but you do not have to look upon its face if you fear to do so. Whether you look upon it or not, visualise it drawing an awesome sword from its side, a sword that appears to be alive with lightning, the living flame in which the Creator manifested in existence. See it raise the sword to its lips and then anoint you with it, touching first the brow or third eye chakra in the centre of the forehead between the eyes, then the left- and right-hand side of the head above the ears, and finally the throat centre.

These points correspond to the Divine centres of Binah, Hokhmah and Daat on the Kabbalistic Tree of Life as they are found on the human body; Binah represents the Divine quality of Understanding, Hokhmah the Divine quality of Wisdom, and Daat the veil through which we receive Higher Knowledge directly from the Divine. Stimulating these energy centres together with the third eye chakra activates and balances a matrix of etheric energy through which we can receive and assimilate knowledge from our guardian angel or Higher Self.

☆ This is the moment to ask specific questions if you require guidance or illumination about something which you do not fully understand.

☆ Next, the Angel of Fire touches the right and left sides of your body from the arms to the hips and down to the legs, neutralising the negative energy in the aura and purifying every cell of your mental, emotional and physical bodies. Feel the flame burning away any centres of disease, numbing any areas of pain, and cauterising any areas of infection.

☆ Now is the moment to ask the Angel of Fire for specific healing if you require it.

☆ Finally, see the sword rise once more and touch each of the seven subtle energy centres (the crown, brow, throat, heart, solar plexus, sacral and root chakras). Sense the living flame coursing through your body to energise you and bring your whole being into balance. When you are ready thank the angel for its blessing and gradually return to waking consciousness.

## The Angel of the Moon

The moon is traditionally a symbol of the mutable feminine principle and of the nocturnal mysteries. Invoking the Angel of the Moon as described in the following exercise is therefore a practical method used by both men and women to focus on and awaken their creative feminine principle, or to explore their latent psychic abilities. Because of the moon's association with the night we can also appeal to this angel to influence our sleep patterns and the content of our dreams. If you have trouble sleeping or are plagued by nightmares, appealing to the Angel of the Moon can help still the mind, calm the emotions and reveal the source of your anxiety.

Working with the Angel of the Moon and the Angel of Water together as described below is particularly effective in dealing with emotional problems, including stress.

When the moon appears spontaneously in meditation it often symbolises the waxing and waning of the unconscious, an indication that the guardian angel or Higher Self is seeking to strengthen contact with the conscious or waking mind. Experience will help you to determine whether the lunar image refers to this awakening or is symbolic of other influences in your life. For example, for a man to see the full moon in meditation or in the dreams which follow might be symbolic of his sister, mother or partner. For a woman a vision of the moon might refer to her mother, a sister or close female friend, although it is more likely to indicate her intensifying intuition.

The appearance of the moon over water during the angel meditation suggests indifference towards someone of emotional significance in your life as the moon is thought to be 'cold'. Alternatively, it could signify that you are under the influence of someone who might be manipulating your emotions for their own interests. Appealing directly to the angel and entrusting it with the problem should resolve the situation or give you the means to resolve it for yourself.

If the moon appears in these meditations as a one-dimensional shape rather than as a planetary body, in an idyllic romantic scenario, it could be that you are being urged to reconsider an emotional attachment which is unrealistic. If so, and the meditation leaves you with a sense that you might have been deceiving yourself in this relationship, then appeal to the Angel of the Moon to free you from the attachment. Visualise the angel wrapping you in its protective wings and unwinding the ties that bind you to this person, and set that person free with love so that he or she will find their true place and their true partner. Then ask the angel to send you whoever has been set aside for the highest good of both of you and imagine this faceless figure being brought from the light towards you. Do not impose a face or any other details on this person, but instead be open to receive what is right for you at this moment in your life.

## EXERCISE: THE ANGEL OF THE MOON

After making yourself comfortable, begin the visualisation as usual by focusing on your breathing.

☆ When you feel suitably relaxed picture yourself in a small chapel or temple, standing or kneeling before an altar which has been dedicated to the Archangel Gabriel who presides over the moon. The altar may be decorated with the appropriate symbols, such as a vase of lilies, a bowl of holy water, a statue of Anubis, the jackal-headed god of ancient Egypt, or a silver chalice. As you contemplate the symbols the moon passes across a stained-glass window above the altar, sending a shaft of light through the window, illuminating you from head to toe.

☆ The light penetrates to the essence of your being. Feel it being absorbed by every cell, and as it does so, feel a sense of detachment as your spirit separates from your physical body and is drawn up the shaft of light.

You are totally absorbed in the light; you and the light are one and there is no longer a sense of self, or of the physical shell into which you were once confined. All anxieties, all physical ailments have been discarded and no longer have any meaning or value for you.

☆ As the intensity of the light diminishes you find yourself outside the chapel or temple in a moonlit woodland. All around you the nature spirits, the minor angelics, are busy with their nightly tasks. They are too preoccupied to pay you any heed as you pass through an avenue of tall, straight trees as if you were walking through a vast palatial hall lined with fluted columns dedicated to the ancient gods and goddesses.

☆ As you reach the apex of this natural and sacred pathway, which follows one of the etheric energy lines of the earth, the moon can be seen framed between the trees. Standing before it is a vast figure overseeing the myriad of natural processes being carried out under its guidance and protection. This is the figure of the Archangel Gabriel to whom you may now appeal for the guidance, strength, healing or assistance that you need.

☆ Once you have made your appeal or asked your question, thank the archangel and return through the avenue of trees to the edge of the wood. There, ask that you may now return to waking consciousness, retaining this sense of oneness with nature and with greater awareness of the unseen processes of life. Then count slowly down from ten to one becoming aware once again of your surroundings, and when you are ready, open your eyes.

# The Angel of the Sun

The sun is traditionally a symbol of the active masculine principle and of the source of all life. Invoking the Angel of the Sun as described in the following exercise is therefore a practical method by which both men and women can focus on and awaken their masculine qualities and stimulate greater awareness, wisdom and spiritual illumination. It can also be an effective symbol for tapping into and absorbing the healing and revitalising energies in the subtle or etheric body.

The spontaneous appearance of the sun in meditation can be symbolic of the need to rest and recuperate, but as with the moon it can also represent a male figure who is a potential source of strength and wisdom. For a woman to have a vision of the sun in meditation might indicate a need to strengthen the relationship with her father, a brother, son or male partner. For a man the sun might symbolise his father, a brother or close male friend, but is more likely to indicate his own increasing awareness of the qualities that he needs to become mature and complete.

The rising sun is also a universal symbol of rebirth and a new phase of life which your guardian angel or Higher Self might project during moments of stillness such as meditation or sleep, to prepare you for the changes to come. In contrast, the setting sun symbolises the conclusion of a particular phase of your life and the need to let go of old attachments.

If you are unsettled because your emotions are preventing you from taking a particular course of action which your intellect considers beneficial, you could be helped by visualising the Angel of the Sun rising over a still lake, its light and energy reflecting in the water. This helps calm the emotions, still the mind and focus the light of the rational mind on the problem.

## EXERCISE: THE ANGEL OF THE SUN – THE CROWNING OF THE SUN KING

Begin as usual by focusing on your breathing.

☆ When you feel sufficiently relaxed visualise yourself stepping into a robe and sandals after a refreshing, scented bath. It is the hour before dawn and you are in an unfurnished antechamber with stained-glass windows which filter the light of the waning moon in such a way as to make you feel that you are stepping through a rainbow. When you have dried and composed yourself for the ceremony to come, you leave the room and enter a vast, vaulted chamber whose floor is chequered with black and white squares denoting the unity of the male and female, active and passive, forces in the universe.

☆ At the far end of the chamber on either side of an ornate bronze throne stand two winged angels bathed in incandescent light. Each is holding the robes and symbols of the sun with which you are to be clothed. They are serene and smiling. On seeing them all your anxieties and feelings of unworthiness are washed away.

☆ You approach and stand before the throne, discarding your robe and stepping out of your sandals as each angel in turn assists you to dress. All the while you look straight ahead, for to gaze into an angel's eyes is only for those who are prepared to have the secrets of their own soul revealed to them.

☆ First, you slip on black shoes symbolic of the physical world, and immediately feel centred and secure.

Then come red breeches representing physical action and strength. You feel the surge of vital energy invigorate every cell of your physical being and send a tingling across your skin. A golden belt is then secured around your waist at which you sense the emotional energy focused in the solar plexus. A green tunic is next, at which your heart centre begins to glow with a warmth which radiates outward through your body. A necklace of blue crystal is fastened around your neck and with it comes a sense that you now have the confidence to express yourself clearly and concisely.

☆ Next, a headband bearing a large precious jewel of violet in an indigo setting is wrapped around your forehead, at which you sense a tingling between the brows. All the energy which has been activated throughout your body is now slowly ascending in a stream of multi-coloured light through the centre of your body to this point, the third eye, the focal point of your psychic sight.

☆ Finally, the angels raise the golden crown and place it gently on your head, at which point the light surges up into your head and saturates your entire being in pure white light.

☆ When you have centred yourself, the angel to your right places the sceptre of the sun in your right hand while the angel on your left offers you the golden orb. Dawn is approaching. You step from the throne and walk out on to the balcony in the company of the angels as the bright burning sun rises before you over the horizon, scattering the stars and rendering the sky aflame. The energy of the sun is yours to command. Ask what you will of the angels and they will assist you. Take what you want from the spirit of the sun for it exists to sustain you. When you have finished your communion with the sun, return to waking consciousness gradually by counting down slowly from ten to one.

A final note on appealing for guidance and help of any kind. It is considered good practice to make your appeal three times, once to inform the conscious mind of your intent, the second time to impress its importance upon the unconscious, and the third time for the ears of the angels.

# 7

# The Angels Within

In *A Book of Angels* the American writer and angel investigator Sophy Burnham spins a wonderful fable which is ostensibly about angels, but in the telling it reveals much about human nature, although she neglects to say whether it is her own story or a traditional tale.

She tells us that when the gods were young they created people for their own amusement, but that these first human beings could not forget where they had come from; all they wanted to do was to return to paradise. So the gods took them back and thought about creating another batch. But first they had to decide where they would hide so that the humans wouldn't find them and spoil the game. If they hid on the moon the humans would eventually develop rockets and search the universe until they found their creators. If they hid in the depths of the ocean, mankind would find ways to explore the abyss and seek them out. The highest mountains and even the centre of the earth would not be safe as long as man remained insatiably curious about his origins and his purpose in the world. Finally, the goddess of wisdom came up with the perfect solution. The gods would hide in the hearts of men because that is the one place they would never think of looking for them.

## The Higher Genius or Guardian Angel

Many scientists, artists and inventors have attributed their insights and inspiration to that mysterious faculty that we call intuition, the instinctive knowledge of something which comes without having to work through the protracted and logical process of reasoning and is not dependent upon perception. The more mystically inclined among them have declared that intuition and inspiration is a form of angelic visitation. The artist and poet William Blake, for example, claimed to have actually seen the angels which brought him the inspiration for his poetry and paintings. 'I am not ashamed to tell you what ought to be told,' he wrote, 'that I am under the direction of messengers from heaven, daily and nightly.'

The more rationally minded have instead credited a nameless higher power or a separate aspect of their own personality with providing the solution that they were seeking. The philosopher Spinoza thought of intuition as the blessing of Divine providence, the Swiss psychoanalyst Carl Jung considered it to come from a contact with the 'collective unconscious', while Albert Einstein professed his openness to higher influence when he remarked, 'The most beautiful and most profound emotion we can experience is the sensation of the mystical. It is the sower of all true science.'

The word 'genius' is commonly used to describe a person of exceptional talent or intellectual ability, but the original meaning of the word (from the Latin *gignere*, 'to beget') referred to each person's guardian spirit. In ancient Rome birthday celebrations would be shared with the person's guardian angel as a mark of respect for the source of their inspiration. This belief in a constant celestial companion as the source of inspiration connects with the concept of a Higher Self or guardian angel, which is today shared by many people of various cultures and creeds. It is my understanding that it was this immortal soul to which Jesus referred when he said, 'The kingdom of heaven is within you', and which Siddhartha Gautama, the Buddha, acknowledged as the Buddha nature in all of us.

The following exercise is designed to help you build a sacred space in the form of a temple on the inner planes, where you can make contact with your Holy Guardian Angel and receive guidance or revitalising and healing energy within the safety of your own energy field, your true field of influence.

## EXERCISE: ANGEL OF THE INNER TEMPLE

☆ Make yourself comfortable with your back straight, your feet flat on the floor and slightly apart and your hands on your thighs.

☆ Close your eyes and begin to focus on your breathing. Take slow, deep, regular breaths. Expel the tension with every out-breath. When you inhale breathe in a golden light which warms and calms you. Feel yourself relaxing with every breath.

☆ Now imagine yourself in the entrance hall or anteroom of a temple. It may be difficult to picture it clearly and in detail at this stage, but it will become more definite, more real in time as you return again and again to create what is in effect your own personal sacred space.

☆ The door to the main inner chamber is before you. What sign is upon the door? A robe hangs on a hook to one side. You change into it and enter the inner chamber. In the centre of the chamber is a pool of still, sparkling water lit from above by a shaft of warm light from a star-crowded night sky streaming in through a skylight. Beyond, in the centre of the far wall, is the door to the North, sealed by a green drape with the symbol of the pentacle. To your right is the door to the West, sealed by a blue drape bearing the symbol of the chalice. To your left is the door to the East, sealed by a yellow drape bearing the symbol of the sword. And behind you closes the door to the South over which hangs a red drape embroidered with the symbol of the rod.

☆ Turning back you see before you on the other side of the pool an altar placed between two pillars. On the altar stand two candle holders in which burn two white candles. Make whatever gestures, offerings or dedications feel right for you to consecrate your actions here and then make your way to the pool. When you are ready, slip off your robe and enter the water. You find the water calming, healing, soothing and strangely invigorating all at the same time. Stress and anxiety are dissolved in the water and washed away as if they were a crusty mud casing so thin you hadn't noticed that it had been clogging up your pores and preventing you from sensing the world around you to full effect. Perhaps there is a perfumed essence in the water or an incense burner on the altar. Whatever the source, you can sense an aromatic essence in the air. What is it?

☆ You wade or swim out to the centre of the pool and are caught in the shaft of light from the skylight. It bathes you in a blissful glow. The colour of the light subtly changes to red, then orange, yellow, green, blue, violet, purple, and finally a brilliant white. The light is so intense that you avoid looking into it and instead avert your gaze into the water. At the same moment you sense a presence drawing near through the light. It is a loving, gentle but intensely powerful presence. You look down into the water and there see the reflection of your Holy Guardian Angel.

☆ It might speak with you. It might leave a gift for you. Do not be overawed or overwhelmed by it; it is a part of you and at the same time it is a discarnate entity. Welcome it, embrace it, speak with it. It comes to help you for your highest good. It comes at your bidding and it will come again whenever you wish to make contact here in the sacred space of the inner temple.

☆ Now it must return, but you will continue to be blessed by its presence long after this experience has ended. It will walk with you and be by your side every moment of your life as it has been thus far, only now you will be more aware of it when you need to be. As speedily as it came it dissolves back into the light and you are left in the glistening pool, invigorated and yet peaceful. Refreshed, you climb out of the pool, put on your robe and if anything has been left for you, a gift or a message, you take that with you back into the antechamber or entrance hall. Here you read the message or ponder the significance of the gift and then change back into your everyday clothes.

☆ Leave the temple when you are ready, thank your angel for its blessing and its presence and then gradually return to normal consciousness and open your eyes.

## The Oversoul

While religious people may talk of conscience or the God within, various schools of esoteric thought have a vague notion of what Ralph Waldo Emerson, the transcendental poet and essayist, called the 'oversoul'; a multi-faceted being from which our individual souls break away and fall to earth like splinters from a shattered crystal. As such we would each be a reflection or facet of that crystal and when, upon death, we return to this greater being as pure consciousness, leaving the shard that was our body behind, we would take with us our experience of the physical world to add to its lustre.

If this were true it might explain why holy men and mystics seem so amused by the intensity of feeling with which their less enlightened fellow beings cling to life and their material possessions. For the real essence of each person, their soul, if you like, would be a mere reflection temporarily animating a physical body, like a spark of electrical current galvanising dead tissue. It would be the physical body's need for form and time which would impose upon us the illusion of reality, but it is this reality that we are conscious of during life as everything is filtered through the physical senses. The greater reality, of which we are an inseparable element, is in effect censored out by the limited perception of the brain, and so we only become aware of the immense and timeless being that we really are when we raise our consciousness through meditation or undergo a spiritual experience which literally takes us out of ourselves.

According to this theory, the concept of a guardian angel

takes on a very different meaning. We and our guardian angels are one and the same; it is simply that we cannot be conscious of more than one aspect of our personality at any one time. When we narrow our vision, so to speak, by focusing on mundane matters, our lower nature takes control, but when we take the blinkers off we are privileged with a wider view, not just the road ahead but the distant horizon and the terrain in between.

Orthodox psychology is inexorably moving towards the acceptance of the presence of the Higher Self which it sees as a multitude of personalities existing within each individual. The branch of psychology known as 'Transactional Analysis', developed by Dr Eric Berne, identifies and acknowledges three types of 'self' within the psyche (he named them Parent, Adult and Child), which take control in turn, depending on the circumstance.

Again, we have Swedenborg's observation on the subject to consider. 'It can in no sense be said that heaven is outside of any one; it is within [...] and a man also, so far as he receives heaven, is a recipient, a heaven, and an angel' (from *Arcano Coelestia*).

Although Swedenborg was convinced of the truth of what he had seen and experienced, he was shrewd enough to know that many of his visionary descriptions would be dismissed out of hand by the public as being the fanciful imaginings of a religious zealot. To that end he qualified what he had described by giving the following advice which all spiritual teachers in the esoteric tradition are duty bound to impart to their pupils. 'Do not believe me simply because I have seen Heaven and Hell, have discoursed with angels [...] Believe me because I tell you what your consciousness and intuitions will tell you if you listen closely to their voice' (from *Angelic Wisdom*).

## EXERCISE: THE ANGEL SANCTUARY

Begin as usual by making yourself comfortable, closing your eyes and focusing on your breathing.

☆ When you feel sufficiently relaxed visualise yourself standing at the edge of a lake in a forest clearing on the far side of which a waterfall cascades down from the hillside sending spray into the air. Even at this distance you can feel the fine droplets on your face as they drift on the breeze, and you can smell the freshness of the water mixed with the scent of pine needles and damp earth.

☆ All is still except for the sound of rushing water and the occasional rustle of leaves as a bird flits from tree to tree. But as you listen you can hear a faint, soft sound as if someone or something is singing from the direction of the waterfall. It is a sweetly seductive sound that calls upon you to enter the water.

☆ Leave your clothes at the water's edge and wade out until it is deep enough to swim. When you reach the far bank you climb out and immerse yourself in the invigorating, cleansing, cascading waters until you feel the cares of the outside world have been washed away and the real you now stands ready to enter the sanctuary that lies behind the waterfall in the hollow of the hillside.

☆ You step through the waterfall into a vast cave, the walls of which glisten and sparkle with the reflected light of natural crystals and precious minerals. The seductive singing has ceased but you can sense the presence of a loving being who wishes you well. At this moment the angel of the lake appears before you. Although it is a supreme spiritual being you are not afraid. The Angel of Water personifies the emotions under control, free from irrational fears and anxieties. It invites you to explore the cave.

☆ Looking around the walls you see empty alcoves to your left. These are the spaces left by the many gifts you have been given in your life so far. Perhaps you can now recall some of the wonderful things that have happened to you which you have not had the time really to consider before now. Perhaps certain events which you believed to have been coincidences are now revealed on reflection to have been help from your angel.

☆ Turning to the opposite wall you find a seemingly endless row of alcoves stretching into the deepest recesses of the cave. The angel tells you that these hold the gifts that are to come, gifts of guidance, insight, natural healing remedies, offers of new opportunities to grow, to satisfy your ambitions and realise your full potential – all for the asking without preconditions or price other than your promise to accept the responsibility that comes with growth. But now, having glimpsed the riches to come, you must return to the outside world and to waking consciousness.

☆ Gradually become aware of your body, your breathing and your surroundings. When you are ready, open your eyes.

## *Past Lives*

In my book *Kabbalah*, I describe a simple exercise for contacting the Higher Self or guardian angel and receiving guidance, which you might find useful. The following exercise is an alternative method which takes the form of a visualisation. It should prove particularly helpful to you in identifying those past lives which have a bearing on your present circumstances, and for clearing any fears, phobias and emotional residue from those previous incarnations. But as with all visualisations it is crucial that you do not allow your ego to deceive you.

First of all, choose a moment when you are in the mood to learn more about yourself, when you are feeling relaxed and receptive and are not simply curious to discover if you were a celebrated historical character. Be aware that it is not you who have been this person from the past, but your Higher Self, of which the conscious 'you' is only a reflection. That past personality has returned to the source and another aspect has incarnated to continue the work of the greater being. You are that new aspect, but you have the ability to draw upon the experience of that past life if you wish to enrich this current incarnation. It is what you learnt from that life for the enrichment of this current incarnation which is important, not the mask that you once wore.

To determine whether an image you receive during meditation is genuine or simply a result of your imagination, ask yourself if it appeared spontaneously and was sustained without any effort on your behalf. Was it similar to watching a film or were you able to manipulate the image? If the image arose spontaneously and could not be altered at will then it may be worth recording. The acid test of any subjective spiritual experience is whether or not it feels true for you. You may receive more pictures of your past life puzzle from a subsequent meditation, or even from your dreams, now that you have made a connection. Consider whatever you receive with a sense of detachment. Try to recall if the images could have been inspired by recent events, perhaps something you've read or seen on a TV programme. If you use your common sense, keep your intentions unsullied by ambition and view everything with interest, keeping your emotions in check, then you won't go far wrong.

The following exercise is called 'The Akashic Angel', after the name given to the matrix of energy on the astral plane which occultists envisage as containing an imprint of every life and event that has taken place on earth. By raising their consciousness to this frequency psychics believe that they can access this 'world memory', as it is sometimes called, and 'read' the record of an individual's past lives.

## EXERCISE: THE AKASHIC ANGEL

First work through the tuning in exercise from Chapter 1 to ground, centre and energise the chakras, then, when you are feeling serene and receptive, affirm to yourself that you wish to learn of your past lives for your own highest good. Now ask your guardian angel for assistance in words of your own choosing.

☆ When you are ready begin to visualise a tiny pinpoint of light in the midst of the blackness. Keep it in focus as you approach it, watching it grow until you find yourself entering a tunnel of incandescent light.

☆ When you emerge from the tunnel you find yourself in a strangely familiar landscape dominated by a vast cathedral-like building made entirely of crystal. This is the Akashic Archive of your own Higher Self, where the records of all of your past lives are stored, not as crumbling parchments and papers, but as living impressions.

☆ Enter the building and take your time to absorb its atmosphere. You note that the interior is illuminated by the light emanating from thousands of stained-glass windows which line the walls and even the ceiling. Those at the entrance depict the angels who have inspired, guided and protected you throughout your many lives and who still watch over you now.

☆ One picture in particular attracts you. You stand before it in silence considering how this particular angel has helped you in the past in ways you were perhaps unaware of at the time. But now you are beginning to sense its presence in your life as it draws closer each day, for it knows that you are becoming more receptive to its influence.

☆ The light from the window is becoming more intense in its brilliance and you turn aside. When you look back, the angel in the window, your guardian angel and the Keeper of the Archives, has materialised before you.

☆ Ask to be shown the record of the past life which has the most relevance to your current situation or concerns and follow your angel to the place where this is kept. Which window does it lead you to? What do you see there? Focus on the image and watch as the past is replayed. Perhaps you are only given a glimpse, a single image or a short scene, and you are not clear which is your part or what relevance it holds for you today. If so, ask your angel to explain it to you, perhaps by letting you see another scene or taking you into the picture to watch as an impartial observer.

☆ The scene may shift several times before you become aware once again of standing at the foot of the window. When you sense that the 'guided tour' is over, thank your angel and ask if you may return again whenever it is necessary.

☆ Finally, before you return to waking consciousness, consider for a few moments that your current incarnation is also leaving an impression in the Akashic record. What impression has it left so far? And what impression would you like it to leave?

☆ When you are ready, return to waking consciousness by counting down slowly from ten to one and recalling your surroundings as you do so.

## A Final Thought

I will leave you with one of my favourite angel stories, a traditional anecdote that requires no further comment.

One night a man was visited by his guardian angel, who took him into the celestial realms to show him scenes from his life so far. As the man watched the events of his life being replayed he noticed that, for most of the journey, there were two sets of footprints on the path where the angel had walked by his side. But at the times of greatest crisis and suffering he was surprised to see only one set of prints. So he said to the angel, 'I thought you were my guardian angel, assigned from my birth to love and protect me, but it seems that when I needed you the most you left me to suffer alone.'

To this the angel gently replied, 'Beloved child, I love you and I would never leave you. During those days and nights when you were burdened by sorrow, worry and fear it was then that I carried you.'

# Useful Addresses

## Angel Websites

### General

http://www.au.spiritweb.org/Spirit/angelic-realms.html
Promoting the spiritual on the Internet since 1993; maintained in Switzerland. E-mail: info@spiritweb.org

http://www.saraharchangels.com/links.htm
Angel Wicca (a pagan site), Archangels, Angel art etc; a long list containing more angel website links.

http://www.rainbowhouse.org/angels.html
(Rainbow House, The Purple Ribbon Project); angel insights, psychic network. E-mail: baangel@flash.net

http://www.tripod.com/bin/search/pursuit
Extensive link list for angel websites, angel poll (an angel popularity poll!), free angel art, books.

http://www.AvatarSearch.com/index/html
Promoting the occult on the Internet.

## *USA*

http://www.ascension-research.org/angelref.html
The Ascension Research Centre, an extremely interesting
site. E-mail: vista@xnet.com

http://www.thepsych.com/category/F50.htm
Angels category from The Internet Psychology Resource.

## *Books and Art*

http://www.eastwest.com/html/Ascended_Masters.htm
Based in California.

http://www.tech-line.com/gta
e-mail: solarlion@lanset.com

http://angelicartistry.com/overview.htm
e-mail: angels@angelicartistry.com

## Angel Workshops

Theolyn Cortens
PO Box 156, Witney, Oxfordshire OX8 8YR

Ruth White
9 Telscombe Grange, 407 South Coast Road, Telscombe Cliffs,
East Sussex BN10 7EY

Diana Cooper
12 Frobisher Gardens, Guildford, Surrey GU1 2NT

# Further Reading

Alma, D., Wyllie, T. and Ramer, A., *Ask Your Angels*, Piatkus, 1992

Bloom, W., *Working with Angels, Fairies and Nature Spirits*, Piatkus, 1998

Burnham, Sophy, *A Book of Angels*, Rider, 1992

Goddard, D., *The Sacred Magic of the Angels*, Samuel Weiser, 1996

Halevi, Z'ev ben Shimon, *A Kabbalistic Universe*, Gateway, 1988

Moolenburgh, Dr H.C., *A Handbook of Angels*, C.W. Daniel, 1988

Moolenburgh, Dr H.C., *Meetings with Angels*, C.W. Daniel, 1992

Price, J. R., *The Angels Within Us*, Piatkus, 1998

Ravenwolf, S., *Angels Companions in Magick*, Llewellyn, 1997

Roland, P., *The Complete Book of Dreams*, Octopus, 1999

Roland, P., *Revelations – The Wisdom of the Ages*, Carlton, 1995

Roland, P., *Kabbalah: A Piatkus Guide*, Piatkus, 1999

Taylor, T. L., *Messengers of Light*, H. J. Kramer Inc, 1990

White, Ruth, *Working With Guides and Angels*, Piatkus, 1996

# Index

# Index